TRUST
LIFE

ALSO BY LOUISE HAY

BOOKS/KIT

The Affirmations Coloring Book (with Alberta Hutchinson)

All Is Well (with Mona Lisa Schulz, M.D., Ph.D.)

The Bone Broth Secret (with Heather Dane)

Colors & Numbers

Empowering Women

Everyday Positive Thinking

Experience Your Good Now!

A Garden of Thoughts: My Affirmation Journal

Gratitude: A Way of Life (Louise & Friends)

Heal Your Body

Heal Your Body A–Z

Heal Your Mind (with Mona Lisa Schulz, M.D., Ph.D.)

Heart Thoughts (also available in a gift edition)

I Can Do It® (book-with-CD)

Inner Wisdom

Letters to Louise

Life Loves You (with Robert Holden)

Life!: Reflections on Your Journey

Love Your Body

Love Yourself, Heal Your Life Workbook

Loving Yourself to Great Health
(with Ahlea Khadro and Heather Dane)

Meditations to Heal Your Life (also available in a gift edition)

Mirror Work

Modern-Day Miracles (Louise & Friends)

The Power Is Within You
Power Thoughts
The Present Moment
The Times of Our Lives (Louise & Friends)
You Can Create an Exceptional Life (with Cheryl Richardson)
You Can Heal Your Heart (with David Kessler)
You Can Heal Your Life (also available in a gift edition)
You Can Heal Your Life Affirmation Kit
You Can Heal Your Life Companion Book

FOR CHILDREN

The Adventures of Lulu (with Dan Olmos)
I Think, I Am! (with Kristina Tracy)
Lulu and the Ant: A Message of Love
Lulu and the Dark: Conquering Fears
Lulu and Willy the Duck: Learning Mirror Work

AUDIO PROGRAMS

All Is Well (audio book)
Anger Releasing
Cancer
Change and Transition
Dissolving Barriers
Embracing Change
The Empowering Women Gift Collection
Feeling Fine Affirmations
Forgiveness/Loving the Inner Child
How to Love Yourself

Meditations for Loving Yourself to Great Health
(with Ahlea Khadro and Heather Dane)
Meditations for Personal Healing
Meditations to Heal Your Life (audio book)
Morning & Evening Meditations
101 Power Thoughts
Overcoming Fears
The Power Is Within You (audio book)
The Power of Your Spoken Word
Receiving Prosperity
Self-Esteem Affirmations (subliminal)
Self-Healing
Stress-Free (subliminal)
The Totality of Possibilities
What I Believe and Deep Relaxation
You Can Heal Your Life (audio book)
You Can Heal Your Life Study Course
Your Thoughts Create Your Life

DVDs

Receiving Prosperity
You Can Heal Your Life Study Course
You Can Heal Your Life, The Movie
(also available in an expanded edition)
You Can Trust Your Life (with Cheryl Richardson)

CARD DECKS

Healthy Body Cards
Heart Thoughts Cards
How to Love Yourself Cards
I Can Do It® Cards
Life Loves You Cards (with Robert Holden)
Power Thought Cards

CALENDAR

I Can Do It® Calendar (for each individual year)

and

THE ESSENTIAL LOUISE HAY COLLECTION
(comprising *You Can Heal Your Life, Heal Your Body,*
and *The Power Is Within You* in a single volume)

All of the above are available at your local
bookstore, or may be ordered by visiting:

Hay House USA: www.hayhouse.com®
Hay House Australia: www.hayhouse.com.au
Hay House UK: www.hayhouse.co.uk
Hay House India: www.hayhouse.co.in

TRUST
LIFE

LOVE YOURSELF EVERY DAY
WITH WISDOM FROM

LOUISE HAY

QUOTES COMPILED BY
ROBERT HOLDEN

HAY HOUSE, INC.
Carlsbad, California • New York City
London • Sydney • New Delhi

Published in the United States by: Hay House, Inc.: www
.hayhouse.com® • *Published in Australia by:* Hay House Australia
Pty. Ltd.: www.hayhouse.com.au • *Published in the United Kingdom by:* Hay House UK, Ltd.: www.hayhouse.co.uk • *Published in
India by:* Hay House Publishers India: www.hayhouse.co.in

Cover design: Karla Baker • *Interior design:* Pamela Homan

Library of Congress Cataloging-in-Publication Data

Names: Hay, Louise L., author.
Title: Trust life : love yourself every day with wisdom from Louise Hay
    / Louise Hay.
Description: Carlsbad, California : Hay House Inc., 2018.
Identifiers: LCCN 2018024477| ISBN 9781401956028 (paperback) | ISBN
    9781401956059 (ebook)
Subjects: LCSH: Self-actualization (Psychology) | Motivation (Psychol-
    ogy) | Affirmations. | BISAC: SELF-HELP / Affirmations. | SELF-HELP /
    Motivational & Inspirational. | SELF-HELP / Personal Growth / Gen-
    eral.
Classification: LCC BF637.S4 H37948 2018 | DDC 155.2--dc23 LC record
    available at https://lccn.loc.gov/2018024477

Tradepaper ISBN: 978-1-4019-5602-8
e-book ISBN: 978-1-4019-5605-9

10 9 8 7 6 5 4 3 2 1
1st edition, October 2018

Printed in the United States of America

FOREWORD

The last time I saw Louise Hay, about a month or so before her death, I shared with her the idea of creating a yearbook featuring daily entries taken from her greatest works. "Oh, I love it!" Louise said excitedly, squeezing both my hands. She looked like a young girl who'd been given a birthday cake. While her body was frail—she was 90 years old, after all—her spirit was radiant and full of purpose.

I shared Louise's excitement. I told her, "A book compiling your favorite teachings is a great way for your readers to experience you every day. They'll be able to have breakfast with you, meditate with you, put you on their bathroom shelf [Louise smiled big when she heard that!], read you on their commute, and take you with them throughout their day."

"You know, I go to bed with millions of people all over the world every night, don't you!" Louise said, with a twinkle in her eye.

"Yes," I said.

"And you know that I also wake up every morning with millions of people, too!" Louise said, referring to the tradition of millions of her fans worldwide who start and end their days with her affirmations, whether written down or in one of her audio programs.

Louise was an icon in the self-help movement for decades, but she never set herself up as an infallible guru with all the answers. In fact, she always stressed that it is *you* who has the power to heal *your* life. She was here only to guide you on the path of remembering the truth of who you are: powerful, loving, and lovable. However, her journey to becoming the "Queen of the New Age," as the *New York Times* dubbed her in 2008, was anything but easy or traditional.

THE PATH TO BECOMING LOUISE HAY

Louise bravely and candidly shared her life story in her books, including being abused by her stepfather, being raped by a neighbor, dropping out of high school, becoming pregnant, and giving up her newborn daughter for adoption on her 16th birthday. "I wasn't brave enough to kill myself, but I used to pray every day that I would die soon," Louise once told me. "My life was very painful, but I managed somehow to bumble along."

She then moved to Chicago, where she took any job she could find. "I ran away from the abuse I experienced at home, but I kept running into more abuse wherever I went," Louise recalled. In 1950 she moved to New York City, where she worked as a high-fashion model for designers like Bill Blass, Pauline Trigère, and Oleg Cassini. While in New York, she met and married Andrew Hay, an English businessman with whom she traveled the world, met royalty, and even had dinner at the White House.

Louise's world fell apart when, after 14 years of marriage, her husband left her for another woman. "I found myself at rock bottom, again!" Louise told me. "That rock bottom was the worst. I wanted nothing more than to crawl under that rock and disappear."

One day, a friend invited Louise to a talk at the First Church of Religious Science. "I nearly didn't go, but I'm glad I did," Louise said. "That night, I heard someone say, 'If you're willing to change your thinking, you can change your life.' Something inside me said, 'Pay attention to this,' and I did."

Overnight, Louise became an avid student of metaphysics and New Thought spirituality. Her favorite authors included luminaries such as Florence Scovel Shinn, Ernest Holmes, and Emmet Fox. "I hadn't read a book in years, but now I was reading every day," she recalled. "I was ready, and when the student is ready, the teachers and the teachings appear." Louise trained as a Religious Science practitioner, then later studied Transcendental

Meditation with Maharishi Mahesh Yogi at his university in Fairfield, Iowa.

At the "School of Religious Science," as Louise called it, she learned a lot about the connection between diseases and the mental patterns that created them. (She always styled *disease* as *dis-ease* to emphasize the connection between a condition and anything that is not in harmony with you or your environment.) Louise began collecting information from the books she read, the people she worked with, and her own thoughts and research. Then, at the urging of many who'd seen her list, she turned her notes into a little blue pamphlet titled *What Hurts*. She initially printed 5,000 copies. "Some of my friends were worried I'd printed 4,000 copies too many and that I wouldn't get my money back!" she told me. Her friends needn't have worried. Her "little blue book," as it affectionately came to be known, sold out in two years. Confident that there was a real need for this information, Louise expanded the material into the book *Heal Your Body*.

It was around this time that Louise was diagnosed with cervical cancer. "Another rock bottom!" she exclaimed. "This time was different, though. My teacher told me, 'Louise, you haven't gone through all this to die now. You have a life to live. It's time to put what you know into practice.' So that's what I did." Louise created a treatment program to help heal her own life. She applied her New Thought principles. She focused on forgiveness. After several months of working with a team of therapists, nutritionists, and bodyworkers, her medical doctor confirmed that her body was free of cancer.

In 1984, Louise founded the company Hay House to self-publish her book *You Can Heal Your Life*. She included material from her little blue book and teachings from her very popular public workshops, as well as stories from her clients and friends. *You Can Heal Your Life* would go on to become a publishing phenomenon. It has sold more than 50 million copies worldwide and made Louise one of the best-selling authors in history—and the fourth best-selling female author after J. K. Rowling, Danielle Steel, and Barbara Cartland. Moreover, it helped to create a new genre of self-help books.

The one thing that Louise may be most remembered for is her pioneering work with men and women living with HIV or AIDS during the epidemic of the 1980s. The medical profession didn't know what to do, and people feared even touching anyone with the dis-ease. People diagnosed with HIV or AIDS were the new outcasts, and they lived in fear, shame, and secrecy. Undeterred, Louise stepped forward and hosted a support group for HIV-positive and AIDS patients every Wednesday night for six and a half years.

"A private client asked me if I'd hold a meeting for men with AIDS. I said yes. That's how it began," Louise told me. Six men showed up for the first meeting, which Louise held in her living room. "I told the men that we were going to do what I always do, which is to focus on self-love, forgiveness, and letting go of fear. I also told them that we were not going to sit there and play *Ain't it awful*, because that won't help anybody."

The weekly meetings soon grew quickly in attendance and became known as the Hayride. "Eventually, we had nearly 90 men squeezed into my living room. I'm not sure what the neighbors thought! Each week we talked, we cried, we sang songs together, we did mirror work and also all sorts of healing meditations for ourselves, each other, and the planet. We ended every evening with hugs, which was good for love and also *very good* for pickups," Louise recalled with a big smile.

Recognizing the need for Louise's work, the city of West Hollywood gave Louise a space that could hold hundreds of people. "Eventually, we had nearly 800 people at our Wednesday night meetings. Now it wasn't just men with AIDS who came. It was men and women. And family members, too. Whenever someone's mother attended her first meeting, she'd receive a standing ovation from us all."

Daniel Peralta, one of Louise's closest friends, first met her in January 1986, when Daniel attended the premiere of a film about the Hayrides called *Doors Opening: A Positive Approach to AIDS*. "Louise Hay introduced me to unconditional love," Daniel once told me. In an article about the Hayrides, Daniel wrote about Louise's infinite kindness and her generosity of spirit: "Louise L. Hay was ushering in a new possibility, a new way of being. She introduced us to loving ourselves and outlined practical steps to engage that process. She gently invited us to be with ourselves in a new and different way, and practice self-acceptance and self-care. Not only was it appealing, it was healing. I clearly remember how Louise had this incredible ability to quickly create a sense of community and bring people together, one heart at a time."

In March 1988, Louise received invitations to appear on both *The Oprah Winfrey Show* and *The Phil Donahue Show*—in the same week! After her daytime TV appearances, her book *You Can Heal Your Life* entered the *New York Times* bestseller list and stayed there for 13 weeks. Louise Hay was now a household name in the U.S. and worldwide.

Luckily, Louise had hired help and incorporated Hay House as a company in 1987; they proved to be equipped for the challenge brought on by her newfound fame! A 25-year-old accountant by the name of Reid Tracy turned out to be a most fortuitous hiring decision. He worked his way up to the role of president of the company in 1998 and helped grow Hay House into an international leader of the healing and self-help movement. The company grew from publishing books to also offering audio recordings, card decks, films, online courses, international workshops, and more. Hay House set up offices in Australia, England, South Africa, and India, so that Louise could feel at home wherever she was in the world.

Although Hay House started by sharing Louise's teachings, they quickly began to welcome others into the family, including leading authors and teachers like Wayne Dyer, Marianne Williamson, Caroline Myss, and Deepak Chopra. In an interview for the Hay House World Summit in 2015, Louise told me, "Of course, I wanted us [Hay House] to be financially successful, so that we could pay wages and look after everyone, but I also had a higher vision. What I knew then, and still believe today, is that the real purpose of Hay House is to help *create a world where it is safe for us to love each other.* With each book we print, we bless the world with love."

In later years, Louise withdrew from the day-to-day running of Hay House and gave more of her attention to her charity, the Hay Foundation, which she founded in 1986. "I see the planet healed and whole, with everyone fed, clothed, housed, and happy," she affirmed, as she set about supporting many worthwhile causes. The Hay Foundation rarely makes public its loving activism in the world. This is how Louise wanted it. Louise was very clear, though, that we heal our life not just for our own benefit but so that we can take our place as a loving presence in the world—someone who loves themselves so that they can love others.

ABOUT THE BOOK IN YOUR HANDS

In honor of Louise's life and work, you now hold in your hands this compilation of her most inspiring teachings from her greatest works. Louise wrote more than 30 books in her lifetime, including self-help books, health books, a cookbook, a children's book series, and even a coloring book! She also co-authored books like *You Can Create an Exceptional Life* with Cheryl Richardson and *Life Loves You* with myself (Robert Holden). She created card decks, audio programs, and an annual *I CAN DO IT!* calendar. My hope is that reading through each day reveals to you the wisdom within each of Louise's works and inspires you to seek out books you haven't yet read.

Trust Life has 365 entries for each day, plus one for each leap year. Each daily entry is titled with a Louise affirmation for you to practice and an inspiring passage for you to meditate on and work with. As I set about choosing each entry, I imagined Louise was sitting with me, just like when we wrote *Life Loves You* together. In fact, I positioned an extra chair next to my writing desk—*the Louise chair*. In my mind, I asked Louise if she was happy with each entry I chose. If I got a *YES,* it was in; if not, it was cut!

Louise was a spiritual pragmatist. She wasn't interested in theory only; she focused on what works and what helps. In *You Can Heal Your Life*, Louise wrote, "I love 'how to's.' All the theory in the world is useless unless we know how to apply it and make a change. I have always been a very pragmatic, practical person with a great need to know how to do things." I have made sure, therefore, that each entry in *Trust Life* offers you a spiritual practice that can make a real difference to how you experience your day.

In *Trust Life*, I wanted to offer a balanced flow *all through the year* between the major themes at the heart of Louise's work. For example, I didn't want to bunch up all the entries on self-love into February or September. *What about self-love for the rest of the year?* To help achieve this balance, I referred to a list I had made of 10 of Louise's core teachings—which I'd shared with Louise's millions of fans in a special tribute on her Facebook page shortly after her death.

My list of 10 Louise Hay teachings isn't meant to be definitive, but I do hope it can be a valuable aid as you work with *Trust Life*.

1. Look in the Mirror

Louise was a pioneer of mirror work: facing yourself in a mirror, looking deeply into your eyes, and repeating positive messages about yourself. If you were a friend of hers, there's a high chance that you would do mirror work together. When we wrote *Life Loves You*, most of our conversations took place in front of a wall-length mirror in Louise's living room.

Louise saw life as a mirror. It mirrors our relationship with ourselves. If we can look in the mirror without judgment or shame, we will see our authentic self, we will forgive ourselves, we will be more loving to others, and we will let Life love us.

Louise recommended mirror work to everyone as the quickest and most effective way of dissolving the blocks to self-love. "When people come to me with a problem—I don't care what it is: poor health, lack of money, unfulfilling relationships, or stifled creativity—there is only one thing that I ever work on, and that is loving the self," wrote Louise in her *Love Yourself, Heal Your Life Workbook*. She encouraged everyone to look in the mirror once a day and say, "I love you, I really love you." "Don't be shy," she'd say. "It's just another way of saying *Life loves you!*"

2. Choose a Heart Thought

Louise was the "queen of affirmations." She saw the world as a state of mind. "The only thing we are ever dealing with is a thought, and a thought can be changed," she wrote in *You Can Heal Your Life*. "No matter what the problem is, our experiences are just outer effects of inner thoughts. Even self-hatred is only a thought you have about yourself."

That is where positive affirmations come in. Whatever we say and think is *affirming* that experience in our lives—and a lot of what we normally say and think is quite negative. When we change our thoughts about ourselves (or someone else), we change our experience of the world. By using positive, first-person statements, we affirm and create more of what we *do* want in our lives. We are retraining our thinking and speaking into patterns we *choose*.

Louise healed her life by changing her thinking. She once told me, "My first affirmation was *I am beautiful, and everybody loves me.* I didn't believe it at first, but I continued to recite it over and over. After three days or so, I noticed that people were being kind to me. I found parking spaces right by where I needed to be. Traffic lights turned green to help me get to places on time. My first affirmation changed the way I experienced my life. It was a miracle."

Louise encouraged all of us to examine our thinking and choose our thoughts. "Think thoughts that work for you!" she said. Choose a heart thought—a loving affirmation—to take with you into your day. Don't just say the affirmation. Sing it out loud. Do it in front of the mirror. Stick it on your refrigerator. Write it on your hand. Live your affirmation like you mean it!

3. Listen to Your Inner Ding

Louise loved to talk about her "inner ding." This was her own affectionate term for her spiritual guidance. "I believe that our minds are always connected to the One Infinite Mind, and therefore, all knowledge and wisdom is available to us at any time. We are connected to this Infinite Mind, this Universal Power that created us, through that spark of light within, our Higher Self, or the Power within," she wrote in *The Power Is Within You*.

Louise learned to live a guided life. She trusted her inner ding. "Ever since I first put my foot onto the spiritual pathway, I felt I had no control over anything, nor did I have to try to control anything. Life has always brought me what I needed. I've always just responded to what showed up," she told Cheryl Richardson in their book *You Can Create an Exceptional Life*.

One of Louise's favorite spiritual practices was to sit quietly, preferably in front of a mirror, connect with her inner ding, and ask, *What would you have me know today?*

4. Forgive Everyone for Everything

"How did Louise Hay become Louise Hay?" I asked her once in an interview.

Louise replied with one word: "Forgiveness."

"I wouldn't be where I am today if I hadn't forgiven the people who have hurt me. I would not want to punish myself today for what they did to me in the past," Louise wrote in *The Power Is Within You*. She defined forgiveness very simply as letting go of the past, describing it as a road to freedom and a necessary "miracle ingredient" for painting your future with bright new colors.

Louise was given a copy of *A Course in Miracles* soon after it was first published and was especially inspired by its teachings on forgiveness. "*A Course in Miracles* says over and over that forgiveness is the answer to almost everything," she wrote in *You Can Heal Your Life*.

5. Be Grateful for Today

I start *Life Loves You* with a story of Louise enjoying a Thanksgiving lunch with her friends to show how gratitude was a daily spiritual practice for Louise—not just an occasional ritual. She began each day by thanking her bed for a good night's sleep! She practiced gratitude mindfully throughout her day. I remember especially how she used to thank her computer, her car, her kettle, and other inanimate objects for working so beautifully. "I enjoy my day more when I remember to be grateful," she told me.

Louise understood that gratitude is an affirmation. The more grateful you are, the more reasons you find to be grateful. Louise kept a gratitude journal for a number of years. "In the evening, just before sleep, I go through the day, blessing and being grateful for each experience. I also forgive myself if I feel that I made a mistake or said something inappropriate or made a decision that was not the best," she wrote in *Gratitude: A Way of Life*.

6. Take Care of Your Body

On the eve of a visit to stay with Louise, I received an email from her: "Bring shorts. You will share my Pilates appointment with Ahlea. Yes, you will. Even if you have to wear MY shorts," she wrote. Ahlea Khadro was Louise's physical therapist and main health caretaker for the last 20 years of Louise's life. She studied nutrition with Ahlea, practiced yoga and Pilates, learned how to make bone broth, and grew organic vegetables and fruits on a small allotment at Ahlea's home. They collaborated on a book with Heather Dane called *Loving Yourself to Great Health*.

Louise taught that your true identity is your inner spirit, not the body. She advocated, however, that it is an act of self-love to care for your body. "Forgive yourself for not treating your body well in the past, and start today to treat your body with love and respect," she taught. One of Louise's favorite affirmations was *I listen with love to my body's messages*. Each day she would take some time to be quiet, tune in to her body, and ask her inner ding, *How can I love my body today?*

7. Create Your Future NOW!

Louise described herself as a late bloomer. She "bumbled along," as she liked to say, well into her late 40s. At 50, she published her first book. At 60, she founded Hay House and the Hay Foundation. The second half of her life was full of new beginnings. At the start of each year, Louise set a conscious intention for her spiritual growth, committed to learning something new, and made plans to travel to somewhere she'd not been before.

Louise embraced her advanced years. She didn't use her age as a reason not to learn and grow. "I live in a *totality of possibilities*," she liked to say. She recognized that each new decade brought its own wisdom and gifts.

"The point of power is always in the present moment," she affirmed.

In 2013, I gave the opening talk at the first *IGNITE!*, a new event by Hay House. The day before, I emailed Louise to ask her if she had a message for the audience. Here's what she sent me:

> *I Ignite my life every time I do something new.*
> *Daring to step into new space is so exciting.*
> *I know that only good lies before*
> *me so I am ready for whatever*
> *Life has in store for me.*
> *New adventures keep us young.*
> *And sending loving thoughts in every direction*
> *keeps our lives filled with love.*
> *86 is the new beginning of my life.*

8. Say YES to Your Life

Louise liked to describe herself as a *yes* person living in a *yes* Universe. In *You Can Heal Your Life* she wrote, "No matter what we choose to believe or think or say, the Universe always says *yes* to us. If we think poverty, the Universe says *yes* to that. If we think prosperity, the Universe says *yes* to that. It's up to us." The message is to be careful what you want to say *yes* to, because you will attract what you affirm.

"All I've ever done is listen to my inner ding and said *yes*," Louise told me as she reflected on her work as an author, speaker, publisher, teacher, artist, and activist. Saying *yes* meant many things for Louise: accepting responsibility for healing her life; being willing to look in the mirror and say, "I love you; I really love you"; being brave enough to write and publish her little blue book; agreeing to host the Hayrides; starting a publishing company; and, above all, trusting in the One Infinite Intelligence to guide her every step of the way.

9. Remember to Have Fun

Louise didn't have much fun in the first half of her life, but she more than made up for it in the second half. This was due, in large part, to the healing work she did with her inner child.

Louise was an advocate of inner child work, which she later called inner child *play*. She taught that a person must be willing to love their inner child if they are to grow into a mature and wise adult. "Say *yes* to your inner child," Louise would say. "Pay attention to her or him. The more you love and accept your inner child, the sooner you will heal your past, step into the present, and come out to play."

At 70, Louise enrolled in a children's art class. "I loved to draw and paint as a young child, but I stopped when the abuse started," she recalled. At 75, Louise graduated to an adult art class. For the next ten years she worked with several art teachers, including local artist Linda Bounds. At 87, Louise held her first public art exhibition at the ArtBeat on Main Street Gallery in downtown Vista, California. The exhibit was hugely popular. The original plan was for a two-week run. It was extended to six weeks. Hundreds of prints were sold, each one signed by Louise, and all the money went to the Hay Foundation.

10. Let Life Love You

On Louise's final appearance on *The Oprah Winfrey Show*, Oprah asked Louise what advice she had for anyone who thinks it's too late to change and grow. Louise responded emphatically, "Rethink! Just because you've believed something for a long time doesn't mean you have to think it forever. Think thoughts that support you and uplift you. Realize that Life loves you. And if you love Life, you get this wonderful thing going."

Life loves you was Louise's signature affirmation. It's the heart thought that best represents her life and work. At her book signings, with lines of hundreds of people, Louise would diligently sign each book with *Life loves you*. She signed off her emails with *Life loves you*. She ended phone calls and Skype sessions with *Life loves you*.

It was always *Life* with a capital "L"—referring to the One Infinite Intelligence at work behind all things.

Life loves you is more than just an affirmation, though. It points to a philosophy of *basic trust* that encourages us to trust that Life—with a capital "L"—wants our highest good, and that the more we love Life, the more Life can love us. The first step on this path of trust is to be willing to let love in. By loving ourselves more, we can truly love one another more. This is how we become a loving presence in the world—someone who affirms wholeheartedly, *I love Life, and Life loves me.*

— Robert Holden
co-author with Louise Hay of *Life Loves You*

EVERY MOMENT OF LIFE IS A NEW BEGINNING POINT

In the infinity of life where I am, all is perfect,
whole, and complete, and yet life is ever changing.
There is no beginning and no end,
only a constant cycling and recycling
of substance and experiences.
Life is never stuck or static or stale,
for each moment is ever new and fresh
I am one with the very Power that created me,
and this Power has given me the power
to create my own circumstances.
I rejoice in the knowledge that I have the power
of my own mind to use in any way I choose.
Every moment of life is a new beginning
point as we move from the old.
This moment is a new point of beginning
for me right here and right now.
All is well in my world.

THIS YEAR I DO THE MENTAL WORK FOR CHANGE

Many of you start New Year's resolutions on the first of the year, but because you don't make internal changes, the resolutions fall away very quickly. Until you make the inner changes and are willing to do some mental work, nothing *out there* is going to change. The only thing you need to change is a thought—only a thought. Even self-hatred is only hating a thought you have about yourself.

What can you do for yourself this year in a positive way? What would you like to do this year that you did not do last year? What would you like to let go of this year that you clung to so tightly last year? What would you like to change in your life? Are you willing to do the work that will bring about those changes?

IT IS SAFE TO LOOK WITHIN

Who are you? Why are you here? What are your beliefs about life? For thousands of years, finding the answers to these questions has meant *going within*. But what does that mean?

I believe there is a Power within each of us that can lovingly direct us to our perfect health, perfect relationships, and perfect careers and that can bring us prosperity of every kind. In order to have these things, we have to believe first that they are possible. Next, we must be willing to release the patterns in our lives that are creating conditions we say we do not want. We do this by going within and tapping the Inner Power that already knows what is best for us. If we are willing to turn our lives over to this greater Power within us, the Power that loves and sustains us, we can create more loving and prosperous lives.

I Am Surrounded by Love

Each one of us has the ability to love ourselves more. Each one of us deserves to be loved. We deserve to live well, to be healthy, to be loved and loving, and to prosper. And that little child within each of us deserves to grow up into a wonderful adult.

So see yourself surrounded by love. See yourself happy and healthy and whole. And see your life as you would like it to be, putting in all the details. Know that you deserve it.

And then take the love from your heart and let it begin to flow, filling your body and then moving out from you. Visualize the people you love sitting on either side of you. Let the love flow to those on your left and send them comforting thoughts. Surround them with love and support, and wish them well. And then let the love from your heart flow to the people on your right. Surround them with healing energies and love and peace and light. Let your love flow around the room until you are sitting in an enormous circle of love. Feel the love circulating as it goes out from you and then comes back to you multiplied.

I Believe in My Power to Change

When you really accept these ideas and make them part of your belief system, you become powerful; then the problems will often solve themselves. The object is to change what you believe about yourself and the world you live in.

1. We are each responsible for our experiences.
2. Every thought we think is creating our future.
3. Everyone is dealing with the damaging patterns of resentment, criticism, guilt, and self-hatred.
4. These are only thoughts, and thoughts can be changed.
5. We need to release the past and forgive everyone.
6. Self-approval and self-acceptance in the "now" are the keys to positive changes.
7. The point of power is always in the present moment.

It is not the people, places, and things that are creating a problem for you; it is how you are "perceiving and reacting" to these life experiences. Take responsibility for your own life. Do not give your power away. Learn to understand more of your inner spiritual-self, and operate under that power that created only good for you.

I CREATE WONDERFUL
NEW BELIEFS FOR MYSELF

Every single thought I have and every sentence I speak is an affirmation. It's either positive or negative. Positive affirmations create positive experiences, and negative affirmations create negative experiences. A tomato seed, if planted, will only grow into a tomato plant. An acorn will only grow into an oak tree. A puppy will only grow into a dog. If we continually repeat negative statements about ourselves or about life, we only keep producing more negative experiences.

I now rise beyond my family habit of seeing life in a negative way. My new affirmation habit is to speak only of the good I want in my life. Then only good will come to me.

LIFE IS REALLY VERY SIMPLE: WHAT WE GIVE OUT, WE GET BACK

What we think about ourselves becomes the truth for us. I believe that everyone, myself included, is responsible for everything in our lives, the best and the worst. Every thought we think is creating our future. Each one of us creates our experiences by our thoughts and our feelings. The thoughts we think and the words we speak create our experiences.

We create the situations, and then we give our power away by blaming the other person for our frustration. No person, no place, and no thing has any power over us, for "we" are the only thinkers in our minds. When we create peace and harmony and balance in our minds, we will find it in our lives.

I Am Beautiful, and
Everybody Loves Me

Mirror work wasn't easy for me in the beginning. The most difficult words for me to say were *I love you, Louise.* I shed a lot of tears, and it took a lot of practice. I had to breathe through my resistance each time I said *I love you* to myself. But I stuck with it. And I'm glad I did, because mirror work has transformed my life.

One day, I decided to try a little exercise. I looked in the mirror and said to myself, "I am beautiful, and everybody loves me." Of course, I didn't believe it at first, but I was patient with myself, and it soon felt easier. Then, for the rest of the day, I said to myself wherever I went, "I am beautiful, and everybody loves me." This put a smile on my face. It was amazing how people reacted to me. Everyone was so kind. That day I experienced a miracle—a miracle of self-love.

I Love and Approve of Myself

Love is the miracle cure. Loving ourselves works miracles in our lives. I am not talking about vanity or arrogance or being stuck-up, for that is not love. It is only fear. I am talking about having a great respect for ourselves and a gratitude for the miracle of our bodies and our minds.

"Love" to me is appreciation to such a degree that it fills my heart to bursting and overflows. Love can go in any direction. I can feel love for:

- the very process of life itself
- the joy of being alive
- the beauty I see
- another person
- knowledge
- the process of the mind
- our bodies and the way they work
- animals, birds, fish
- vegetation in all its forms
- the Universe and the way it works

What can you add to this list?

I GENTLY GUIDE MY MIND TOWARD
TRUSTING MY OWN INNER WISDOM

No person, place, or thing has any power over me, for I am the only thinker in my mind. As a child, I accepted authority figures as gods. Now I am learning to take back my power and become my own authority figure. I now accept myself as a powerful, responsible being. As I meditate every morning, I get in touch with my own inner wisdom. The school of life is deeply fulfilling as we come to know that we are all students and all teachers. We each have come to learn something and to teach something. As I listen to my thoughts, I gently guide my mind toward trusting my own inner wisdom. Grow and blossom and entrust all your affairs on Earth to your Divine Source. All is well.

I Cherish My Body and Take Care of It Well

It's an act of love to take care of your body. As you learn more and more about nutrition, you'll start to notice how you feel after you eat certain foods. You'll figure out which foods give you optimum strength and lots of energy. Then, you'll stick to eating those foods.

We need to cherish and revere these wonderful temples that we live in. I believe the best way to be good to your body is to remember to love it. Look into your own eyes in the mirror often. Tell yourself how wonderful you are. Give yourself a positive message every time you see your own reflection. Just love yourself. Don't wait until you become thinner or more muscular or until you lower your cholesterol levels. Just do it now. Because you deserve to feel wonderful all the time.

I Am Willing to Love Myself

Practice this mirror work exercise throughout the day. You can begin in the morning in front of your bathroom mirror, and then during the day you can repeat it whenever you pass a mirror or see your reflection in a window.

1. Stand or sit in front of your mirror.

2. Look into your eyes.

3. Take a deep breath and say this affirmation: *I want to like you. I want to really learn to love you. Let's go for it and really have some fun.*

4. Take another deep breath and say, *I'm learning to really like you. I'm learning to really love you.*

5. This is the first exercise, and I know it can be a little challenging, but please stay with it. Keep taking deep breaths. Look into your eyes. Use your own name as you say, *I'm willing to learn to love you, [Name]. I'm willing to learn to love you.*

6. Throughout the day, each time you pass a mirror or see your reflection, please repeat these affirmations, even if you have to do it silently.

PERFECT HEALTH IS MY DIVINE RIGHT, AND I CLAIM IT NOW

I believe that we contribute to every "illness" in our body. The body, as with everything else in life, is a mirror of our inner thoughts and beliefs. Our body is always talking to us, if we will only take the time to listen. Every cell within our bodies responds to every single thought we think.

When we discover what the mental pattern is behind an illness, we have a chance to change the pattern and, therefore, the dis-ease. Most people do not want to be sick on a conscious level, yet every dis-ease that we have is a teacher. Illness is the body's way of telling us that there is a false idea in our consciousness. Something that we are believing, saying, doing, or thinking is not for our highest good. I always picture the body tugging at us saying, "Please pay attention!"

Every Day Is a New Beginning for Me

Today is a new day. Today is a day for you to begin creating a joyous, fulfilling life. Today is the day to begin to release all your limitations. Today is the day for you to learn the secrets of life. You can change your life for the better. You already have the tools within you to do so. These tools are your thoughts and your beliefs.

Every thought you think and every word you speak is an affirmation. All of our self-talk, our internal dialogue, is a stream of affirmations. You're using affirmations every moment, whether you know it or not. You're affirming and creating your life experiences with every word and thought.

An affirmation opens the door. It's a beginning point on the path to change. In essence, you're saying to your subconscious mind: "I am taking responsibility. I am aware that there is something I can do to change." Consciously choose words that will either help eliminate something from your life or help create something new in your life.

*Today I create a wonderful new day
and a wonderful new future.*

*Each day is a new opportunity. Yesterday is over
and done. Today is the first day of my future.*

I feel safe in the rhythm and flow of ever-changing life.

I RECOGNIZE THE
MAGNIFICENCE OF MY BEING

How perfect you were when you were a tiny baby. Babies do not have to do anything to become perfect; they already are perfect, and they act as if they know it. They know they are the center of the Universe. They are not afraid to ask for what they want. They freely express their emotions. You know when a baby is angry—in fact, the whole neighborhood knows. You also know when babies are happy, for their smiles light up a room. They are full of love.

Tiny babies will die if they do not get love. Once we are older, we learn to live without love, but babies will not stand for it. Babies also love every part of their bodies, even their own feces. They have incredible courage.

You were like that. We were all like that. Then we began to listen to adults around us who had learned to be fearful, and we began to deny our own magnificence.

I never believe it when clients try to convince me how terrible they are or how unlovable they are. My work is to bring them back to the time when they knew how to really love themselves.

I Embrace My Inner
Child with Compassion

I have found that working with the inner child is most valuable in helping to heal the hurts of the past. We are not always in touch with the feelings of the frightened little child within us. If your childhood was full of fear and battling, and you now mentally beat yourself up, you are continuing to treat your inner child in much the same way. The child inside, however, has no place to go. You need to go beyond your parents' limitations. You need to connect with the little lost child inside. He or she needs to know that you care.

Take a moment now and tell your child, "I care. I love you. I really love you." Maybe you've been saying this to the big person, the adult inside you. So start talking to the little child. Visualize that you are taking him or her by the hand and go everywhere together for a few days, and see what wonderfully joyous experiences you can have.

I See Myself through the Eyes of Love

"The first time I did mirror work was not easy," Louise says.

"What happened?" Robert Holden asks.

"I looked for flaws. And I found plenty of them!" she says with a smile. "Oh, my eyebrows weren't right. I had too many wrinkles. My lips weren't the right shape. There was a long list."

"Were you tempted to stop doing the mirror work?"

"Yes, but I had a good teacher who I trusted, and he helped me to feel safe in front of the mirror. He pointed out to me that the mirror wasn't judging me; it was *me* who was judging me. Therefore, I didn't need to be afraid of the mirror."

"So, you stuck with the mirror work."

"Yes, and after a while I began to notice the little miracles," says Louise.

"What do you mean?"

"Well, traffic lights seemed to turn green just for me. And good parking spaces would appear in places that were normally impossible. I was in the rhythm of life. I was easier on myself, and life was getting easier."

I Am Willing to Forgive Everyone and Everything

Whenever we are ill, we need to search our hearts to see who it is we need to forgive.

A Course in Miracles says, "All dis-ease comes from a state of unforgiveness," and "Whenever we are ill, we need to look around to see who it is that we need to forgive."

I would add to that concept that the very person you find it hardest to forgive is the one *you need to let go of the most*. Forgiveness means giving up, letting go. It has nothing to do with condoning behavior. It's just letting the whole thing go. We do not have to know *how* to forgive. All we need to do is to be *willing* to forgive. The Universe will take care of the hows.

I Trust Life to Bring Me Everything I Need

Years ago, I had a friend who invited me to a lecture at a Church of Religious Science in New York. She asked me to join her because she didn't want to go by herself. I agreed, but when I arrived, she wasn't there. I was left to decide whether or not to attend by myself, and I decided to stay.

So there I was, sitting in this lecture, when I heard someone say, "If you are willing to change your thinking, you can change your life." While it sounded like a small, tiny statement, it was huge to me. It caught my attention. I have no idea why, because I was a person who never studied anything. I remember having a friend who kept trying to get me to go to the YWCA for classes, and I wasn't interested. But something about this subject spoke to me at that time, and I made a decision to go back.

I can now see the perfection in my friend not showing up. If she had, I probably would have had a different experience. You see, everything is perfect.

I SEE THE WORLD ENVELOPED IN A CIRCLE OF LOVE

See yourself standing in a very safe space. Release your burdens and pain and fear. Release old, negative patterns and addictions. See them falling away from you. Then see yourself standing in your safe place with your arms wide open, saying, *I am open and receptive*—willing to declare for yourself what you want, not what you don't want. See yourself whole and healthy and at peace. See yourself filled with love.

And in this space, feel your connection with other people in the world. Let the love in you go from heart to heart. And as your love goes out, know that it comes back to you multiplied. Send comforting thoughts to everyone and know that these comforting thoughts are returning to you.

On this planet, we can be in a circle of hate, or we can be in a circle of love and healing. I choose to be in a circle of love. I realize that we all want the same things: to be peaceful and safe, and to express ourselves creatively in ways that are fulfilling.

See the world becoming an incredible circle of love. And so it is.

A LOVING WORLD STARTS WITH ME

I want to help create a world where it is safe for us to love each other, where we can express who we are and be loved and accepted by the people around us without judgment, criticism, or prejudice.

Loving begins at home. The Bible says, "Love thy neighbor as thyself." Far too often we forget the last couple of words—*as thyself.* We really can't love anyone out there unless the love starts inside us. Self-love is the most important gift we can give ourselves, because when we love who we are, we will not hurt ourselves, and we will not hurt anyone else. With inner peace, there would be no wars, no gangs, no terrorists, and no homeless. There would be no dis-ease, no AIDS, no cancer, no poverty, and no starvation.

So this, to me, is a prescription for world peace: to have peace within ourselves. Peace, understanding, compassion, forgiveness, and, most of all, love. We have the Power within us to effect these changes.

I Love Myself as I Am Right Now

The Power that created this incredible Universe has often been referred to as love. *God is love.* We have often heard the statement: *Love makes the world go 'round.* It's all true. Love is the binding agent that holds the whole Universe together.

To me, love is a deep appreciation. When I talk about loving ourselves, I mean having a deep appreciation for who we are. We accept all the different parts of ourselves—our little peculiarities, the embarrassments, the things we may not do so well, and all the wonderful qualities, too. We accept the whole package with love. Unconditionally.

Unfortunately, many of us will not love ourselves until we lose the weight, or get the job, or get the raise, or the boyfriend, or whatever. We often put conditions on our love. But we can change. We *can* love ourselves as we are right now!

I Can Choose My Thoughts

Louise and Robert Holden were out for a walk one day, following a nature trail near her home. Big old eucalyptus trees shaded them from the bright sun. They got talking about the principle *You can choose your thoughts*.

"What exactly does this principle mean?" he asked Louise.

She said, "It means thoughts have no power other than what you give them." Thoughts are just ideas—possibilities in consciousness—that are only big or powerful if we identify with them. "You are the only thinker in your mind, and you can choose if your thoughts are true or not."

One of Robert's favorite Louise Hay principles is *The only thing we are ever dealing with is a thought, and a thought can be changed*. Most of the time when we are in pain, it's because we are responding to our thoughts about something. The pain is mind made. It is a sign that we are literally suffering from psychology. The way out of suffering is to make friends with your mind and remind yourself that you are the thinker of your thoughts. Happiness is only ever one thought away.

I Am Worthy of My Own Love

The more you practice mirror work, the easier it will get. But remember that it is going to take time. That's why I'd like you to get into the habit of doing your mirror work frequently. Do it when you first get up in the morning. Carry a pocket mirror wherever you go, so you can take it out often and say a loving affirmation to yourself.

1. Stand in front of a mirror.

2. Look into your eyes.

3. Using your name, say this affirmation: *[Name], I love you. I really, really love you.*

4. Take a few moments now to say it two or three more times: *I really, really love you, [Name].*

5. Keep repeating this affirmation over and over. I want you to be able to say it at least 100 times a day. Yes, that's right: 100 times a day. I know that seems like a lot, but honestly, 100 times a day is easy once you get into the swing of it.

6. So each time you pass a mirror or see your reflection, just repeat this affirmation: *[Name], I love you. I really, really love you.*

I LOVE AND ACCEPT MYSELF EXACTLY AS I AM

I love and accept myself exactly as I am. I support myself, trust myself, and accept myself wherever I am. I can be within the love of my own heart. I place my hand over my heart and feel the love that is there. I know there is plenty of room for me to accept myself right here and now. I accept my body, my weight, my height, my appearance, my sexuality, and my experiences. I accept all that I have created for myself—my past and my present. I am willing to allow my future to happen.

I am a Divine, Magnificent Expression of Life, and I deserve the very best. I accept this for myself now. I accept miracles. I accept healing. I accept wholeness. And most of all, I accept myself. I am precious, and I cherish who I am. And so it is.

ALL MY NEEDS ARE MET AT ALL TIMES

The Power that created us has put everything here for us. It is up to us to deserve and to accept. Whatever we have now is what we have accepted. If we want something different or more or less, we don't get it by complaining; we can only get something different by expanding our consciousness. Welcome all your bills with love, and rejoice as you write out the checks, knowing that what you're sending out is coming back to you multiplied. Start feeling positive about this issue. Bills are really wonderful things. It means that somebody has trusted you enough to give you their service or product, knowing that you have the ability to pay for it.

The One Infinite Intelligence
Always Says *Yes* to Me

I know that I am one with all of Life. I am surrounded by and permeated with Infinite Wisdom. Therefore, I rely totally on the Universe to support me in every positive way. Everything I could possibly need is already here waiting for me. This planet has more food on it than I could possibly eat. There is more money than I could ever spend. There are more people than I could ever meet. There is more love than I could possibly experience. There is more joy than I can even imagine.

The One Infinite Intelligence always says yes *to me. No matter what I choose to believe or think or say, the Universe always says* yes. *I do not waste my time on negative thinking or negative subjects. I choose to see myself and Life in the most positive ways. I say* yes *to opportunity and prosperity. I say* yes *to all good. I am a* yes *person living in a* yes *world, being responded to by a* yes *Universe; and I rejoice that this is so. I am grateful to be one with Universal Wisdom and backed by Universal Power. Thank you, God, for all that is mine to enjoy in the here and now.*

I LOVINGLY CREATE
PERFECT HEALTH FOR MYSELF

I am one with Life, and all of Life loves me and supports me. Therefore, I claim for myself perfect, vibrant health at all times. My body knows how to be healthy, and I cooperate by feeding it healthy foods and beverages, and exercising in ways that are enjoyable to me. My body loves me, and I love and cherish my precious body. I am not my parents, nor do I choose to re-create their illnesses. I am my own unique self; and I move through life healthy, happy, and whole. This is the truth of my being, and I accept it as so. All is well in my body.

I SPARKLE AND GLOW WHEREVER I GO

My body is perfect for me at this time. My body weight is also perfect. I am exactly where I choose to be. I am beautiful, and every day I become more attractive. This concept used to be very hard for me to accept, yet things are changing now that I am treating myself as if I were someone who was deeply loved. I'm learning to reward myself with healthy little treats and pleasures now and again. Little acts of love nurture me, doing things that I really like, such as quiet time, a walk in nature, a hot soothing bath, or anything that really gives me pleasure. I enjoy caring for myself. I believe it is okay to like myself and to be my own best friend. I know my body is filled with starlight and that I sparkle and glow everywhere I go.

I Speak to Myself with Love

The best way to love yourself is to release all the negative messages from your past and live in the present moment. Often, early messages from parents, teachers, and other authority figures contribute to your self-talk—what you say to yourself in your head. So with this mirror work exercise, I'd like you to change your self-talk.

1. Stand or sit in front of your mirror.
2. Look into your eyes.
3. Say this affirmation: *Whatever I say to myself, I will say it with love.*
4. Keep repeating it: *Whatever I say to myself in this mirror, I will say it with love.*
5. Is there a statement that you heard as a child that still sticks in your head? "You're stupid" or "You're not good enough." Take time to work with negative statements and turn them into positive affirmations: *I am a Genius with an abundance of creative ideas. I am a magnificent person. I am worth loving.*
6. Choose one or two of these new, positive affirmations and say them over and over again. Keep saying them until you feel comfortable with them.
7. Each time you pass a mirror or see your reflection in a window throughout the day, stop and repeat these loving affirmations.

I LISTEN WITH LOVE TO MY BODY'S MESSAGES

Let's discover the power of written affirmations! Writing an affirmation can intensify its power. Write a positive affirmation about your health 25 times. You may create your own, or use one of the following:

My healing is already in process.
I listen with love to my body's messages.
My health is radiant, vibrant, and dynamic now.
I am grateful for my perfect health.
I deserve good health.

I Open Myself to the Wisdom Within

In the infinity of life where I am,
all is perfect, whole, and complete.
I believe in a power far greater than I am
that flows through me every moment of every day.
I open myself to the wisdom within, knowing that
there is only One Intelligence in this Universe.
Out of this One Intelligence comes all the answers, all
the solutions, all the healings, all the new creations.
I trust this Power and Intelligence, knowing that
whatever I need to know is revealed to me,
and that whatever I need comes to me
in the right time, space, and sequence.
All is well in my world.

I Am Loving and Lovable and Loved

I believe each one of us decides to incarnate upon this planet at particular points in time and space. We have chosen to come here to learn a particular lesson that will advance us on our spiritual, evolutionary pathway.

One of the ways to allow the process of life to unfold for you in a positive, healthy way is to declare your own personal truths. Choose to move away from the limiting beliefs that have been denying you the benefits you so desire. Declare that your negative thought patterns will be erased from your mind. Let go of your fears and burdens. For a long time now, I have been believing the following ideas, and they have worked for me:

1. "Everything I need to know is revealed to me."
2. "Everything I need comes to me in the perfect time-space sequence."
3. "Life is a joy and filled with love."
4. "I am loving and lovable and loved."
5. "I am healthy and filled with energy."
6. "I prosper wherever I turn."
7. "I am willing to change and to grow."
8. "All is well in my world."

My Higher Self Is Immune to Manipulation and Guilt

"Helping people to heal guilt is the most important work I do," says Louise. "As long as you believe you are unworthy and keep making yourself guilty, you stay stuck in a story that does no one any good at all."

Robert Holden asks Louise if guilt has any positive purpose. She replies, "The only positive function of guilt is that it tells you you've forgotten who you really are and that it's time to remember." Guilt is a warning sign, an alarm that sounds when you are not in alignment with your true nature and acting with love.

"Guilt doesn't heal anything," says Louise.

"Explain that, please," he asks.

"Feeling guilty about what you did, or what someone did to you, doesn't make the past go away. Guilt doesn't make the past better."

"Are you saying we should never feel guilt?"

"No," says Louise. "I'm saying that when you feel guilt or believe that you are unworthy, you should use it as a sign that you need to heal."

"How do we heal guilt, Louise?"

"Forgiveness."

My Business Is Doing What I Love

I trust Divine Intelligence to run my business. Whether I own my own business in a worldly sense or not, I am an instrument employed by this Divine Intelligence. There is only One Intelligence, and this Intelligence has a splendid track record in the history of our solar system, guiding each of the planets for millions of years along pathways that are orderly and harmonious. I willingly accept this Intelligence as my partner in business. It is easy for me to channel my energy into working with this Powerful Intelligence. Out of this Intelligence comes all the answers, all the solutions, all the healings, all the new creations and ideas that make my business such a joyous blessing and success.

I TRUST THE PROCESS OF MY LIFE

Ever since I first put my foot onto the spiritual pathway, I felt I had no control over anything, nor did I have to try to control anything. Life has always brought me what I needed. I've always just responded to what showed up. So often people ask about how I started Hay House. They want to know every detail from the day I began up to today. My answer is always the same: I answered the phone and opened the mail. I did what was before me.

That's how I lived. It was as if Life simply took care of everything one step at a time. So the business started first with me and my then-90-year-old mother, who was very good at sealing envelopes and licking stamps, and it grew from there.

ABUNDANCE FLOWS INTO MY LIFE IN SURPRISING WAYS EVERY DAY

The first time I heard the concept "The abundance of the Universe is available to everyone," I thought it was ridiculous.

"Look at all the poor people," I said to myself. "Look at my own seemingly hopeless poverty." To hear "Your poverty is only a belief in your consciousness" only made me angry. It took me many years to realize and accept that I was the only person responsible for my lack of prosperity. It was my belief that I was "unworthy" and "not deserving," that "money is difficult to come by" and "I do not have talents and abilities," that kept me stuck in a mental system of "not having."

Money is the easiest thing to demonstrate! How do you react to this statement? Do you believe it? Are you angry? Are you indifferent? Are you ready to throw this book across the room? If you have any of these reactions—*good*! I have touched something deep inside you, that very point of resistance to truth. This is the area to work on. It is time to open yourself to the potential of receiving the flow of money and all good.

I Trust My Inner Wisdom

Listening to your inner guidance and acting on it is the way to health and happiness. Remember, you are the first step in your health, and your immune system is learning from your ability to care for yourself. Your cells are learning from what you think and believe. Affirm:

I love and care for my inner child.
I trust my inner wisdom. I say no when I want
to say no, and I say yes when I want to say yes.
I am guided throughout this
day in making the right choices.
Divine Intelligence continuously guides
me in the realization of what is right for me.
As I go about my day, I listen to my own guidance.
My intuition is always on my side.
I trust it to be there at all times. I am safe.
I speak up for myself. I ask for
what I want. I claim my power.

LIFE SUPPORTS AND LOVES ME

When people come to me with a problem, I don't care what it is—poor health, lack of money, unfulfilling relationships, or stifled creativity—there is only one thing I ever work on, and that is *loving the self*.

I find that when we really love and accept and *approve of ourselves exactly as we are*, then everything in life works. It's as if little miracles are everywhere. Our health improves, we attract more money, our relationships become much more fulfilling, and we begin to express ourselves in creatively fulfilling ways. All this seems to happen without our even trying.

My Day Begins and
Ends with Gratitude

Guess what Louise Hay does first thing when she wakes up each morning? Well, it's not brushing her teeth or going to the toilet. And it's not dancing the rumba. I'm not saying she doesn't do any of those things each morning, but it's not what she does first thing.

"On waking, before I open my eyes, I like to thank my bed for a good night's sleep," says Louise.

"Louise, you're the only person I know who thanks her bed for a good night's sleep," Robert Holden tells her.

"Well, I'm pleased for you that you've finally met someone who does," she says.

"It's not very normal, is it?" he jests.

"I'm not interested in being normal," she counters.

"Normal is overrated," he says.

"I think so," says Louise.

"So when did you first start to thank your bed for a good night's sleep?"

"Oh, I don't know," she says, as if she's been doing it forever.

"Was it 30 years ago, 40 years ago?"

"Once upon a time I used to wake up and think, *Oh shit! Another day!*" she says with a big laugh.

"Now that's a powerful affirmation!"

I Love My Family
Members Just as They Are

Children are not the parents' possessions; they are blessings from the Universe. They are individual bright spirits, old spiritual souls coming to have another human experience. They have chosen their parents for the lessons and challenges they will be given. They are here to teach us many things if we are open to learning from them. Children are challenging, for they often have different ways of looking at Life. Parents frequently insist on teaching them old, outdated ideas that the children instinctively know are not right for them. It is the parents' duty to provide a safe, nurturing space for this soul to develop its current personality to the fullest.

If we only could realize that each child who comes to this planet is a healer and could do wondrous things to advance humanity if it is but encouraged. When we try to force a child into a mold that was passed down from our grandparents, then we do the child a disservice, and we do society a disservice.

I Bless This Situation with Love

The most powerful tool that I can share with you to transform any situation is the power of blessing with love. No matter where you work or how you feel about the place, bless it with love. I mean this literally. Don't just think positive thoughts in a vague way. Instead, say, "I bless this job with love." Find a place where you can say this out loud—there is so much power in giving voice to love. And don't stop there. Bless everything in your workplace with love: the equipment, the furniture, the machines, the products, the customers, the people you work with and for, and anything else associated with your job. It works wonders.

I ACCEPT ONLY KIND AND LOVING PEOPLE IN MY WORLD

The ending of a relationship is difficult for most of us to handle. We often give our power over to the other person, feeling that he or she is the source of the love we feel. Then, if that person leaves, we are devastated. We forget that love lies within us. We have the power to choose our feelings. Remember, no person, place, or thing has any power over us. Bless the other person with love and release him or her.

Some of us are so starved for love that we will endure a poor relationship just to be with someone, anyone. We all need to develop so much self-love that we only attract to ourselves people who are there for our highest good.

We must all refuse to accept abuse of any sort. To accept it only tells the Universe that such is what we believe we deserve, and as a result, we will get more of it. Affirm for yourself: *I accept only kind and loving people in my world.*

LIFE LOVES ME UNCONDITIONALLY

Notice that the affirmation *Life loves you* is only three words long. There are no other words. It's not *Life loves you because . . .* For example, *because I am a good person*, or *because I work hard*, or *because I just got a raise*, or *because my football team won*. Similarly, it's not *Life will love you if . . .* For example, *if I lose 10 pounds*, or *if I heal this cancer*, or *if I find a girlfriend*. *Life loves you* is about unconditional love.

When you feel lovable, you experience a world that loves you. The world is a mirror. There is no real difference between saying to yourself *I love you* and *Life loves you*. It's all the same love. When you let life love you, you feel lovable; and when you feel lovable, you let life love you. Now you are ready to be who you really are.

FEBRUARY 14

I Am Very Thankful for All the Love in My Life

Allow these affirmations to fill your consciousness, knowing they will become true for you. Practice them often, with joy:

- *From time to time, I ask those I love how I can love them more.*
- *I choose to see clearly with eyes of love. I love what I see.*
- *I draw love and romance into my life, and I accept it now.*
- *Love is around every corner, and joy fills my entire world.*
- *I rejoice in the love I encounter every day.*
- *I am comfortable looking in the mirror and saying, "I love you. I really, really love you."*
- *I now deserve love, romance, joy, and all the good that Life has to offer me.*
- *I am surrounded by love. All is well.*
- *I am beautiful, and everybody loves me.*
- *I am greeted by love wherever I go.*
- *I attract only healthy relationships. I am always treated well.*
- *I am very thankful for all the love in my life. I find it everywhere.*

I Love Myself and My Sexuality

People often equate sex with love, or they need to be in love to have sex. Many of us grew up believing that sex was sinful unless we were married, or that sex was for procreation and not for pleasure. Some people have rebelled against this concept and feel that sex has nothing to do with love.

Most of our beliefs about sex can be traced to our childhood and our ideas about God and religion. Most of us were raised with the idea of what I call "Mama's God," which is what your mother taught you about God when you were very little. It is often the image of God as an old man with a beard. This old man sits on a cloud and stares at people's genitals, waiting to catch someone sinning.

Think for a moment about the vastness of the Universe. How perfect it all is! Think about the level of Intelligence that created it. I have a difficult time believing that this same Divine Intelligence could resemble a judgmental old man watching my genitals.

When we were babies, we knew how perfect our bodies were, and we loved our sexuality. Babies are never ashamed of themselves. No baby ever measures its hips to find its self-worth.

I Choose Love Instead of Fear

In any given situation, I believe that we have a choice between love and fear. We experience fear of change, fear of not changing, fear of the future, and fear of taking a chance. We fear intimacy, and we fear being alone. We fear letting people know what we need and who we are, and we fear letting go of the past.

At the other end of the spectrum we have love. Love is the miracle we are all looking for. Loving ourselves works miracles in our lives. I am not talking about vanity or arrogance, for that is not love. That is fear. I am talking about having a great respect for ourselves and a gratitude for the miracle of our body and our mind.

I Am Willing to Forgive
Everyone to Set Myself Free

No matter what avenue of spirituality you follow, you will usually find that forgiveness is an enormous issue at any time, but most particularly when there is an illness. When we are ill, we really need to look around and see who it is we need to forgive. And usually the very person who we think we will never forgive is the one we need to forgive the most. Not forgiving someone else doesn't harm the person in the slightest, but it plays havoc with us. The issues aren't theirs; the issues are ours.

The grudges and hurts you feel have to do with forgiving yourself, not someone else. Affirm that you are totally willing to forgive everyone: *I am willing to free myself from the past. I am willing to forgive all those who may ever have harmed me, and I forgive myself for having harmed others.* If you think of anyone who may have harmed you in any way at any point in your life, bless that person with love and release him or her, then dismiss the thought.

I Release My Anger and Set Myself Free

Don't swallow your anger and have it settle in your body. When you get upset, give yourself a physical release. There are several methods you can use to release these feelings in positive ways. You can scream in the car with the windows closed. You can beat your bed or kick pillows. You can make noise and say all the things you want to say. You can scream into a pillow. You can run around a track, or play a game like tennis to release the energy. Beat the bed or kick pillows at least once a week, whether you feel angry or not, just to release those physical tensions you store in your body!

I Am Open and Receptive to the Healing I Need

See a new door opening to a decade of great healing —healing that we have not understood in the past. We are in the process of learning about all the incredible abilities that we have within ourselves. And we are learning to get in touch with those parts of ourselves that have the answers and are there to lead us and guide us in ways that are for our highest good.

See this new door opening wide and imagine stepping through it to find healing in many, many different forms, for healing means different things to different people. Some of us have bodies that need healing; some of us have hearts that need healing; some of us have minds that need healing. So we are open and receptive to the healing that each person needs. We open the door wide for personal growth, and we move through this doorway knowing we are safe. And so it is.

IT IS BECOMING EASIER FOR ME TO MAKE CHANGES

You are much more than your mind. You may think your mind is running the show, but that is only because you have trained your mind to think in this way. You can also untrain and retrain this tool of yours.

Your mind is a tool for you to use in any way you wish. The way you now use your mind is only a habit, and habits, any habits, can be changed if we want to do so, or even if we only know it is possible to do so.

Quiet the chatter of your mind for a moment, and really think about this concept: *your mind is a tool you can choose to use any way you wish.*

The thoughts you "choose" to think create the experiences you have. If you believe that it is hard or difficult to change a habit or a thought, then your choice of this thought will make it true for you. If you would choose to think, *It is becoming easier for me to make changes*, then your choice of this thought will make that true for you.

I Create Wonderful New Beliefs for My Life

Just as a mirror reflects your image, your experiences reflect your inner beliefs. When something uncomfortable is happening, look inside and ask, *How am I contributing to this experience? What is within me that believes I deserve this? How can I change this belief?*

1. Stand in front of a mirror. Take a deep breath and, as you exhale, allow all tension to leave your body.

2. Look at your forehead and imagine all the old beliefs and negative thoughts playing in your head. Reach up and imagine pulling these words out of your head and throwing them away.

3. Now look deeply into your eyes and tell yourself, *Let's make a new recording of positive beliefs and affirmations.*

4. Say these affirmations aloud: *I am willing to let go. I release all tension. I release all fear. I release all anger. I release all guilt. I release all sadness. I let go of old limitations and beliefs. I am at peace with myself. I am at peace with the process of life. I am safe.*

5. Repeat these affirmations two or three times.

6. Throughout the day, whenever any difficult thoughts arise, take out your pocket mirror and repeat these affirmations.

I Choose to Love and Enjoy Myself

When you're in a state of anxiety or fear that keeps you from functioning, you may have abandoned your inner child. Think of some ways in which you can reconnect with your inner child. What could you do for fun? What could you do that is just for you?

List 15 ways in which you could have fun with your inner child. You may enjoy reading good books, going to the movies, gardening, keeping a journal, or taking a hot bath. How about some "childlike" activities? Really take the time to think. You could run on the beach, go to a playground and swing on a swing, draw pictures with crayons, or climb a tree. Once you've made your list, try at least one activity each day. Let the healing begin!

Look at all you've discovered! Keep going—you can create such fun for you and your inner child! Feel the relationship between the two of you healing.

I Bless All My
Friendships with Love

Friendships can be our most enduring and important relationships. We can live without lovers or spouses. We can live without our primary families, but most of us cannot live happily without friends. I believe that we choose our parents before we are born into this planet, but we choose our friends on a more conscious level.

Friends can be an extension or a substitute for the nuclear family. There is a great need in most of us to share life experiences with others. Not only do we learn more about others when we engage in friendship, but we can also learn more about ourselves. These relationships are mirrors of our self-worth and esteem. They afford us the perfect opportunity to look at ourselves, and the areas where we might need to grow.

When the bond between friends becomes strained, we can look to the negative messages of childhood. It may be time for mental housecleaning. Cleaning the mental house after a lifetime of negative messages is a bit like going on a good nutritional program after a lifetime of eating junk foods. As you change your diet, the body will throw off a toxic residue, and you may feel worse for a day or two. But you can do it! I know you can!

I AM A BELOVED
CHILD OF THE UNIVERSE

We are all beloved children of the Universe, and yet there are dreadful things happening, such as child abuse. It is said that 30 percent of our population has experienced child abuse. This is not something new. We are at a point right now where we are beginning to allow ourselves to be aware of things that we used to conceal behind walls of silence. These walls are starting to come down so that we can make changes. Awareness is the first step in making changes. For those of us who had really difficult childhoods, our walls and our armors are very thick and strong. Still, behind our walls, the little child in each one of us just wants to be noticed and loved and accepted exactly as is—not changed or made different.

No matter what happened in the past, begin now to allow the tiny child inside to blossom and know that it is deeply loved. Affirm: *It is safe for me to grow up.*

I Know That Life Always Supports Me

Bo [Robert Holden's daughter] loves to read stories first thing in the morning and just before bedtime. Two books in her collection are children's books written by Louise Hay. One is *I Think, I Am!*, which teaches kids about the power of affirmations. The other is *The Adventures of Lulu*, which is a collection of stories that help children to feel confident and be creative.

"Lulu is the girl I'd like to have been when I was growing up," says Louise. "She knows that she is lovable and that life loves her."

Lulu and Bo are a similar age. They both have blonde hair. Each has a little brother. Sometimes they get afraid. Sometimes they get hurt. And life teaches them how to listen to their heart and live with courage. There's a verse in one of Lulu's songs that says:

You can be what you want to be,
you can do what you want to do,
you can be what you want to be,
    all of Life supports you.

I Now Live in Limitless Love, Light, and Joy

As you read this, take a deep breath and, as you exhale, allow all the tension to leave your body. Let your scalp and your forehead and your face relax. Your head does not need to be tense in order for you to read. Let your tongue and your throat and your shoulders relax. You can hold a book with relaxed arms and hands. Do that now. Let your back and your abdomen and your pelvis relax. Let your breathing be at peace as you relax your legs and feet.

Is there a big change in your body since you began the previous paragraph? Notice how much you hold on. If you are doing it with your body, you are doing it with your mind.

In this relaxed, comfortable position, say to yourself, "I am willing to let go. I release. I let go. I release all tension. I release all fear. I release all anger. I release all guilt. I release all sadness. I let go of all old limitations. I let go, and I am at peace. I am at peace with myself. I am at peace with the process of life. I am safe."

I Let Go of Old, Negative Patterns with Ease

How did you experience love as a child? Did you observe your parents expressing love and affection? Were you raised with lots of hugs? Or in your family, was love expressed through fighting, yelling, crying, door-slamming, manipulation, control, silence, or revenge? If it was, then you'll most likely seek out similar experiences as an adult. You'll find people who will reinforce those ideas. If, as a child, you looked for love and found pain, then as an adult, you'll find pain instead of love . . . unless you release your old family patterns.

I Love My Children, and They Love Me

Affirmations for My Children

I communicate openly with my children.
My children are Divinely protected.
I have a loving, harmonious, joyous, healthy family.
My children are safe and secure wherever they go.
I have a loving, peaceful
relationship with my children.
My children grow strong and love themselves.
I accept and cherish my children's uniqueness.
I allow my children to express themselves freely.
I love my children, and they love me.
We are all a part of the family of love.

MY HOME IS A WONDERFUL
PLACE TO LIVE IN

Look at your home. Is it a place where you really want to live? Is it comfortable and joyous, or is it cramped and dirty and always messy? If you don't feel good about it, you are never going to enjoy it. Your home is a reflection of you. What state is it in? Clean out your closets and refrigerator. Take all the stuff in the closets that you haven't worn in a period of time and sell it, give it away, or burn it. Get rid of it so that you can make room for the new. As you let it go, say: "I'm cleaning out the closets of my mind." Do the same with your refrigerator. Clean out all the foods and scraps that have been there for a while.

People who have very cluttered closets and cluttered refrigerators have cluttered minds. Make your home a wonderful place to live in.

I TRUST LIFE ALWAYS WANTS
WHAT IS BEST FOR ME

In the infinity of life where I am,
all is perfect, whole, and complete.
I am always Divinely protected and guided.
It is safe for me to look within myself.
It is safe for me to look into the past.
It is safe for me to enlarge my viewpoint of life.
I am far more than my
personality—past, present, or future.
I now choose to rise above my personality problems
to recognize the magnificence of my being.
I am totally willing to learn to love myself.
All is well in my world.

I Have Come to This
Planet to Learn to Love

We are in the midst of enormous individual and global change. I believe that all of us who are living at this time chose to be here to be a part of these changes, to bring about change, and to transform the world from the old way of life to a more loving and peaceful existence.

In the Piscean Age we looked "out there" for our savior: "Save me. Save me. Please take care of me." Now we are moving into the Aquarian Age, and we are learning to go within to find our savior. We are the power we have been seeking. We are in charge of our lives.

If you are not willing to love yourself today, then you are not going to love yourself tomorrow, because whatever excuse you have today, you'll still have tomorrow. Maybe you'll have the same excuse 20 years from now, and even leave this lifetime holding on to the same excuse. Today is the day you can love yourself totally with no expectations.

EVERYTHING IS WORKING OUT FOR MY HIGHEST GOOD

You can ask Life to help you in any situation. Life loves you and is there for you, if only you'll ask. Look in the mirror and ask Life, "What do I need?" Listen for the answer, a feeling, or whatever comes up. If nothing comes up in that moment, be open to an answer coming at a later time. And affirm:

Life loves me.
I trust things to be wonderful.
I observe with joy as Life
abundantly supports and cares for me.
I know that only good awaits me at every turn.
All is well. Everything is working out for my highest good.
Out of this situation only good will come.
I am safe.

I Am Blessed

Louise begins her day with gratitude. "It's a great way to start the day," she says. However, she doesn't just do a 10-minute gratitude exercise and then get busy with her day. She makes a point of taking gratitude with her into her day. She has reminders everywhere. Underneath the mirror that hangs on her kitchen wall there's a sign in gold lettering that reads *What are you grateful for today?* Louise practices gratitude with great mindfulness, and she happily expresses her gratitude to everyone and to everything.

"Louise, I've been watching you!" Robert Holden says. "And I see that you are in constant dialogue with life. You talk to your bed. You talk to your mirror. You talk to your teacup. You talk to your breakfast bowl. You talk to your computer. You talk to your car. You talk to your clothes. You talk to everything."

"Yes, I do," she says with pride.

"And mostly what you say is 'Thank you.'"

"Well, I'm grateful that my car works well, and that my computer connects me to my friends, and that my clothes feel so nice to wear."

"I think you live an enchanted life," he says.

"I am blessed," she says.

I Release All Self-Criticism Now

Most of us have such a strong habit of judgment and criticism that we cannot easily break it. It is also the most important issue to work on immediately. We will never be able to really love ourselves until we go beyond the need to make life wrong.

As a little baby you were so open to life. You looked at the world with eyes of wonder. Unless something was scary or someone harmed you, you accepted life just as it was. Later, as you grew up, you began to accept the opinions of others and to make them your own. You learned how to criticize.

Perhaps you were led to believe that you need to criticize yourself in order to grow and change. I do not agree with that concept at all!

I believe that criticism shrivels our spirits. It only enforces the belief that "we are not good enough." It certainly does not bring out the best in us.

I Am Perfect Exactly as I Am

You are neither too much nor too little. You do not have to prove to anyone or anything who you are. You are the perfect expression of the oneness of life. In the infinity of life you have been many identities, each one a perfect expression for that particular lifetime. Be content to be who and what you are in this life. Do not yearn to be like someone else, for that is not the expression you chose this time. Next time you will be different. You are perfect as you are, right here and right now. You are sufficient. You are one with all of Life.

There is no need to struggle to be better. All you need to do is to love yourself more today than yesterday and to treat yourself as someone who is deeply loved. Love is the nourishment that humans need to fulfill their greatness. As you learn to love yourself more, you learn to love everyone more.

Together we lovingly nourish an ever more beautiful world. We are all healed, and the planet is healed, too. With joy, we recognize our perfection and the perfection of Life. And so it is.

I Am a Loving Presence in the World

I think it's time for us to move away from our limited thinking and to develop a more cosmic view of life. The community of human beings on planet Earth is opening up on a scale that has never been seen before. New levels of spirituality are connecting us. We are learning on a soul level that we are all one. We have chosen to incarnate at this time for a reason. I believe we have chosen on a deep level to be a part of the healing process of the planet.

Remember that every time you think a thought, it goes out from you and connects with like-minded people who are thinking the same thing. We can't move to new levels of consciousness if we remain stuck in old judgments, prejudices, guilt, and fears. As we each practice unconditional love of ourselves and others, the entire planet will heal.

I Love and Support and Enjoy the Women in My Life

In honor of International Women's Day, choose affirmations that empower you as a woman (or give these affirmations below as a gift to yourself and to the women in your life).

I love being a woman.
I see within myself a magnificent being.
I love and appreciate myself.
I am a powerful woman,
infinitely worthy of love and respect.
I am wise and beautiful.
I am free to be all that I can be.
I am subject to no one; I am free.
I choose to love and enjoy myself.
I love, and support, and enjoy the women in my life.
I am safe, and all is well in my world.

I CO-CREATE MY LIFE
WITH MY HIGHER SELF

The creativity of the Universe flows through me all day long, and all I have to do to participate in it is to know that I am a part of it. It is easy to recognize creativity when it comes in the form of a painting, a novel, a movie, a new wine, or a new business. Yet I am creating my entire life every moment from the most common, ordinary creation of new cells in my body—from choosing my emotional responses, to my parents and their old patterns, to my present job, my bank account, my relationships with friends, and my very attitudes about myself.

One of my most powerful gifts is my imagination. I use it to see good things happening to me and to everyone around me. I am peaceful as I co-create my life with my Higher Self.

I Am Surrounded by Good Drivers

Let's use driving as an example of one way to start your day differently. First of all, have your car be a friend. Talk to it nicely. I often say, "Hi, darling, how are you, so nice to see you. We're going to have a nice ride to the office."

You might even name your car—I do. And when I leave my home, I affirm: *I am surrounded by good drivers*, and I make sure to send love into all the cars around me. I always like to feel that there's love everywhere on the road.

Other affirmations you can use when driving are:

My ride is easy and effortless.
My drive goes smoothly, and more quickly than I expect.
I feel comfortable in the car.
I know this will be a beautiful drive to the office [or to school, the store, or the like].
I bless my car with love.
I send love to every person on the road.

I Trust the Wisdom of My Inner Self

There is a place within each of us that is totally connected with the infinite wisdom of the universe. In this place lie all the answers to all the questions we will ever ask. Learn to trust your inner self.

As I go about my daily affairs, I listen to my own guidance. My intuition is always on my side. I trust it to be there at all times. I am safe.

I RELEASE ALL RESENTMENT AND SET MYSELF FREE

There is an old Emmet Fox exercise for dissolving resentment that always works. He recommends that you sit quietly, close your eyes, and allow your mind and body to relax. Then, imagine yourself sitting in a darkened theater, and in front of you is a small stage. On that stage, place the person you resent the most. It could be someone in the past or present, living or dead. When you see this person clearly, visualize good things happening to this person—things that would be meaningful to him. See him smiling and happy.

Hold this image for a few minutes, then let it fade away. I like to add another step. As this person leaves the stage, put yourself up there. See good things happening to you. See yourself smiling and happy. Be aware that the abundance of the Universe is available to all of us.

I RELEASE THE PAST WITH EASE AND FORGIVE EVERYONE

Healing is a release from the past. Everyone's past includes some disaster and pain. There is only one way to survive your past, and that is to practice forgiveness. Without forgiveness, you can't get past your history. You feel stuck. Your life isn't moving on, because you haven't moved on. The present can't comfort you because you're not really here. The future looks like more of the same because you only see your past. In reality, the past is over, but it isn't over in your mind. That's why you're still in pain.

Until you forgive, you will keep giving your future to the past. However, forgiveness teaches you that who you truly are has nothing to do with what happened in your past. Your experiences are not your identity. They can have a big effect on you, but they do not define you. What you did to another person or what they did to you is not the end of your story. When you can say, "I am not my past" and "I am willing to forgive my past," you can create a new future. With forgiveness, a new chapter begins.

I LOVINGLY CREATE MY OWN REALITY

Emotional problems are among the most painful of all. Occasionally we may feel angry, sad, lonely, guilty, anxious, or frightened. When these feelings take over and become predominant, our lives can become an emotional battleground.

We need to realize that it doesn't matter what anybody else did to us or what we were taught in the past. Today is a new day. We are now in charge. Now is the moment in which we can create the future for ourselves. We definitely can, because we have a Higher Power within that can help us break free from these patterns if we will allow it to happen.

Affirmations for Emotional Health

I now live in limitless love, light, and joy.
All is well in my world.
I claim my own power, and I lovingly create my own reality.
My level of understanding is constantly growing.
I am in the process of positive change.
I love and approve of myself.
I trust Life, and I am safe.
I accept my uniqueness.
It is safe to look within.
Life supports me.

I CHOOSE TO SEE
CLEARLY WITH EYES OF LOVE

Today, put all criticism and negative self-talk aside. Let go of your old mind-set—the one that berates you and resists change. Release other people's opinions of you. Affirm: *I am good enough. I am worth loving.*

1. Stand in front of a mirror.
2. Look into your eyes.
3. Say this affirmation: *I love and approve of myself.*
4. Keep saying it over and over again: *I love and approve of myself.*
5. Repeat this affirmation at least 100 times a day. Yes, that's right: 100 times. Let *I love and approve of myself* become your mantra.
6. Each time you pass a mirror or see your reflection, repeat this affirmation.

This is an exercise I have given to hundreds and hundreds of people over the years. The results are absolutely phenomenal when people stick with it. Remember: mirror work doesn't work in theory; it only works in practice. If you do it, it really will make a difference.

I Accept Health as the Natural State of My Being

In the infinity of life where I am,
all is perfect, whole, and complete.
I accept health as the natural state of my being.
I now consciously release any mental patterns
within me that could express as dis-ease in any way.
I love and approve of myself.
I love and approve of my body.
I feed it nourishing foods and beverages.
I exercise it in ways that are fun.
I recognize my body as a wondrous and magnificent machine,
and I feel privileged to live in it.
I love lots of energy.
All is well in my world.

MY MIND IS A GARDEN FULL OF BEAUTIFUL THOUGHTS

Think of your mind as if it were a garden. To begin with, a garden is a patch of dirt. You may have a lot of brambles of self-hatred and rocks of despair, anger, and worry. An old tree, called fear, needs pruning. Once you get some of these things out of the way, and the soil is in good shape, you add some seeds or little plants of joy and prosperity. The sun shines down on it, and you water it and give it nutrients and loving attention.

At first, not much seems to be happening. But you don't stop; you keep taking care of your garden. If you are patient, the garden will grow and blossom. It's the same with your mind—you select the thoughts that will be nurtured, and with patience they grow and contribute to creating the garden of experiences you want.

MY LIFE IS UNFOLDING
IN GLORIOUS WAYS

Today is the only opportunity you will ever have to experience this day. Stay in the now, and rejoice in every moment. Don't let your days slip by in frustration or you will miss out on much of your joy. Take a month of expressing gratitude at every turn. Life loves a grateful person and gives even more to be grateful for. Affirm: *My life is unfolding in glorious ways. I am at peace.*

WHEREVER I LOOK, I SEE BEAUTY

Beauty is everywhere. Natural beauty shines forth from every little flower, from the patterns of reflected light on the surface of water, from the quiet strength of old trees. Nature thrills me, renews and refreshes me. I find relaxation, enjoyment, and healing in the simplest things in life. As I look with love at nature, I find it easy to look with love at myself. I am part of nature; therefore, I am beautiful in my own unique way. Wherever I look, I see beauty. Today I resonate with all the beauty in life.

I Am a Beautiful Unique Soul

Part of self-acceptance is releasing other people's opinions. If I were with you and kept telling you, "You are a purple pig, you are a purple pig," you would either laugh at me or get annoyed with me and think I was crazy. It would be most unlikely that you would think it was true. Yet many of the things we have chosen to believe about ourselves are just as far-out and untrue. To believe that your self-worth is dependent on the shape of your body is your version of believing that "you are a purple pig."

Often what we think of as the things "wrong" with us are only our expressions of our own individuality. This is our uniqueness and what is special about us. Nature never repeats itself. Since time began on this planet, there have never been two snowflakes alike or two raindrops the same. And every daisy is different from every other daisy. Our fingerprints are different, and we are different. *We are meant to be different. When we can accept this, then there is no competition and no comparison.* To try to be like another is to shrivel our soul. We have come to this planet to express who *we are.*

I Express Gratitude and Thanksgiving Every Day, in Every Way

"Guess what I do last thing at night," says Louise, with a twinkle in her eye.

"What do you do?" Robert Holden asks.

"I go to bed with thousands of people all over the world," she says, laughing.

"How do you do that?"

"People take me to bed with them!" she says.

"How lovely!"

"They download me so that we can lie in bed and meditate together before going to sleep," she explains.

"Louise Hay, you are full of mischief!"

"Guess what else I do before I go to sleep?"

"I can't imagine," he says.

"I go through my day, blessing and being grateful for each experience," she tells me.

"Do you do this in bed?"

"Yes, mostly. The other night I opened up my pocket mirror—the one you gave me with the inscription *Life Loves You*—and I said my gratitudes out loud to the mirror."

I AM ONE WITH ALL LIFE, AND ALL OF LIFE LOVES AND SUPPORTS ME

We are in partnership with Divine Intelligence. We are not interested in the negative aspects of the outer world, for they have nothing to do with us. We expect, and we receive, positive results. We attract to ourselves only those in the world who operate on the highest level of integrity.

Everything we do is done in the most positive way. We are constantly grateful for the opportunities that are presented to us to help this planet and each person on it. We go within and connect with our higher intelligence, and we are always led and guided in ways that are for the highest benefit of all concerned.

We are all healthy and happy. Everything is in harmony and flows in Divine right order. All is well. We know this to be true for us.

I Drop the Word *Should*
from My Vocabulary

Most of us have foolish ideas about who we are and many rigid rules about how life should be lived. Let's remove the word *should* from our vocabulary forever. *Should* is a word that makes prisoners of us. Every time we use *should*, we are making ourselves wrong or someone else wrong. We are, in effect, saying: *not good enough.*

What can be dropped now from your *should* list? Replace the word *should* with the word *could*. *Could* lets you know that you have a choice, and choice is freedom. We need to be aware that everything we do in life is done by choice. There is really nothing we *have* to do. We always have a choice.

MARCH 24

Whatever I Need to Know Is Revealed to Me in the Perfect Time-Space Sequence

I really know that there is a Power far greater than myself that flows through me every moment of every day, and I can open myself to this Power and receive what I need, whenever I choose. This is true of everyone. We all are learning that it is safe to look within. It is safe to enlarge our viewpoint of life. If things aren't going the way we expected in some area, it doesn't mean we are bad or wrong. It is a signal that we are being redirected by Divine Guidance. When this happens, find a quiet place where you can relax and connect with the Intelligence within you. Affirm that the supply of wisdom is inexhaustible and available to you, and that whatever you need to know is revealed to you in the perfect time-space sequence.

I ALWAYS SPEAK TO MYSELF
IN A KIND AND LOVING WAY

I well remember my first lecture. When I came down from the podium, I immediately said to myself, "Louise, you were wonderful. You were absolutely fantastic for the first time. When you have done five or six of these, you will be a pro."

A couple of hours later, I said to myself, "I think we could change a few things. Let's adjust this, and let's adjust that." I refused to criticize myself in any way.

If I had come off the podium and begun berating myself with "Oh, you were so awful. You made this mistake, and you made that mistake," then I would have dreaded my second lecture. As it was, the second one was better than the first, and by the sixth one, I was feeling like a pro.

I AM OPEN AND RECEPTIVE TO DIVINE GUIDANCE TODAY

I am constantly increasing my understanding. I am teachable. Every day I open my awareness a little more to the Divine Wisdom within me. I am glad to be alive and so grateful for the good that has come to me. Life, to me, is an education. Every day I open my mind and my heart and discover new insights, new people, new viewpoints, and new ways to understand what's happening around and within me. The more I understand, the more my world expands. My new mental skills are really helping me feel more at ease with all the changes in the incredible school of life here on planet Earth.

I Am Forgiving, Loving, Gentle, and Kind, and I Know That Life Loves Me

"Forgiveness taught me that as much as I wanted my past to be different, it was over now," Louise says. "Through forgiveness, I was able to use my past to learn, to heal, to grow, and to take responsibility for my life now." What really makes a difference in your life is not what happened in the past but what you do with your past in the present. "The present moment is your point of power," says Louise. "You can create only in this moment now." With forgiveness, you change your relationship to the past, and this changes your relationship to the present and the future.

"The present is forgiveness," states *A Course in Miracles*. In the present moment, we let go of the past. In the present moment, we fear nothing. In the present moment, there is no guilt. In the present moment, the meaning of the past can be undone. In the present moment, a new future is born. With forgiveness, we remember the basic truth *I am lovable*. With forgiveness, we let life love us. With forgiveness, we can be a loving presence to the people in our life.

IT IS SAFE FOR ME TO RELEASE MY INNER CRITIC AND MOVE INTO LOVE

By doing mirror work, you will become more aware of your inner voice and what you say to yourself. Then you'll be able to release the need to pick on yourself all the time. And when you do, you will notice that you no longer criticize others so much.

When you make it okay to be yourself, then you automatically allow others to be themselves. Then, as you stop judging others, they release the need to judge you. Everybody gets to be free.

1. Find a quiet place with a mirror where you will feel safe and where you won't be disturbed.

2. Look into the mirror. Look straight into your eyes. If you are still uncomfortable doing this, then concentrate on your mouth or your nose. Talk to your inner child. Your inner child wants to grow and blossom, and needs love, acceptance, and praise.

3. Now say these affirmations: *I love you. I love you, and I know you are doing the best you can. You are perfect just as you are. I approve of you.*

4. You may want to do this exercise several times before you truly feel that your inner voice is less critical. Do what feels right for you.

I TRUST THAT LIFE WANTS THE BEST FOR ME

Trust is what we learn when we want to overcome our fears. It's called taking the leap of faith. Trust in the Power within that is connected to the Universal Intelligence. Remember, the Power that supplies your breath is the same Power that created the Universe. You are one with all of Life. The more you love yourself and trust Life, the more Life is here to love you, support you, and guide you. You can trust in that which is invisible, instead of trusting only in the physical, material world. I'm not saying that we do nothing, yet if we have trust, we can go through life much easier. We need to trust that we are being taken care of, even though we're physically not in control of everything that is happening around us.

I LISTEN WITH LOVE TO MY INNER CHILD

One of the first statements that you can make when you first talk to your child is an apology. Say you are sorry that you haven't talked to it in all these years, or that you are sorry for scolding it for so long. Tell the child that you want to make up for all the time spent apart from one another. Ask it how you can make it happy. Ask the child what frightens him or her. Ask how you can help, and ask what it wants from you.

Start out with simple questions; you will get the answers. *What can I do to make you happy? What would you like today?* For instance, you can say to the child, "I want to jog; what do you want to do?" He or she may answer, "Go to the beach." The communication will have begun. Be consistent. If you can take just a few moments a day to begin to connect with the little person inside of you, life is going to be a lot better.

I MOVE THROUGH FORGIVENESS TO LOVE

Affirmations for Forgiveness

The door to my heart opens inward.
I move through forgiveness to love.
As I change my thoughts, the world around me changes.
The past is over, so it has no power now.
The thoughts of this moment create my future.
It is no fun being a victim. I refuse to be
helpless anymore. I claim my own power.
I give myself the gift of freedom from
the past and move with joy into the now.
There is no problem so big or so
small that it cannot be solved with love.
I am ready to be healed, I am
willing to forgive, and all is well.
I know that old, negative patterns no
longer limit me. I let them go with ease.
As I forgive myself, it becomes easier to forgive others.
I forgive myself for not being perfect.
I am living the very best way I know how.
It is now safe for me to release all of my
childhood traumas and move into love.
I forgive everyone in my past for all
perceived wrongs. I release them with love.
All of the changes in life that lie
before me are positive ones, and I am safe.

I AM WILLING TO BEGIN
WHERE I AM RIGHT NOW

In the infinity of life where I am,
all is perfect, whole, and complete.
The past has no power over me because
I am willing to learn and to change.
I see the past as necessary
to bring me to where I am today.
I am willing to begin where I am right now
to clean the rooms of my mental house.
I know it does not matter where I start, so I now
begin with the smallest and the easiest rooms,
and in that way I will see results quickly.
I am thrilled to be in the middle of this
adventure, for I know I will never go
through this particular experience again.
I am willing to set myself free.
All is well in my world.

I Am Willing to Let
Life Love Me Today

"*Life loves you* is a beautiful affirmation," Robert Holden says, "but it's more than just an affirmation."

Louise gives one of her knowing smiles. "I hope so," she says. "*Life loves you* offers us a basic philosophy for living. These three words are a signpost that points us to the heart of creation, to our relatedness to each other, and to our true nature. *Life loves you* shows us who we are and how to live a truly blessed life."

"What does *Life loves you* mean to you, Louise?" he asks.

"Life loves us *all*. It doesn't just love you or me," she replies.

"So we are all included."

"Life loves all of us," she repeats.

"Love must include us all, or else it is not love."

"Yes, and no one is more special than anyone else."

"We are all equals in the eyes of love."

"Yes, and no one is left out."

"No unholy exceptions!"

I Create a Loving Atmosphere around Myself

Dis-ease is related to a resistance to the flow of Life in some areas, and to the inability to forgive. I forgive myself for not treating my body well in the past. Now I care enough for myself to nourish myself with all the best that Life has to offer. It is my body and my mind, and I am in charge. I help my body, my mind, and my spirit live healthfully by creating a loving atmosphere around myself. I now choose the peaceful, harmonious loving thoughts that create an internal atmosphere of harmony for the cells in my body. I love every part of my body. Life is good, and I enjoy living it!

I AM A KIND AND LOVING FRIEND TO MYSELF

I am one with Life, and all of Life loves and supports me. Therefore, I claim for myself emotional well-being at all times. I am my best friend, and I enjoy living with myself. Experiences come and go, and people come and go, but I am always here for myself. I am not my parents, nor their patterns of emotional unhappiness. I choose to think only thoughts that are peaceful, joyous, and uplifting. I am my own unique self, and I move through life in a comfortable, safe, and peaceful way. This is the truth of my being, and I accept it as so. All is well in my heart and my mind.

My Income Is Constantly Increasing

I allow my income to constantly expand, no matter what the newspapers and economists say. I move beyond my present income, and I go beyond the economic forecasts. I don't listen to people out there telling me how far I can go or what I can do. I easily go beyond my parents' income level. My consciousness of finances is constantly expanding and taking in new ideas—new ways to live deeply, richly, comfortably, and beautifully. My talents and abilities are more than good enough, and it is deeply pleasurable for me to share them with the world. I go beyond any feelings that I do not deserve, and I move into acceptance of a whole new level of financial security.

OUT OF THIS SITUATION
ONLY GOOD WILL COME

When we are in a state of overwhelm, it is good to stop focusing on the negative. We can never find a good solution when we only see limitations. Take a deep breath. Let your shoulders, face, and scalp relax. Turn the whole situation over to the Universe. Say to yourself repeatedly: *All is well. Everything is working for our highest good. Out of this situation only good will come. We are safe!*

Then focus on what you could envision as the perfect solution. What is the ideal scene? Put your intentions down on paper. Hold to this vision. Do constant positive affirmations. Then relax and let the Universe work out how they will manifest.

I Know Today Is Going to Be a Really Good Day

My first thoughts on awakening before I open my eyes are to be thankful for everything I can think of. After a shower, I take half an hour or so to meditate and do my affirmations and prayers. Then after about 15 minutes of exercise, usually on the trampoline, I will sometimes work out with the 6 A.M. aerobic program on television.

Now I'm ready for breakfast. I thank the Earth Mother for providing this food for me, and I thank the food for giving its life to nourish me. Before lunch, I like to go to a mirror and do some affirmations out loud; I may even sing them—something like:

Louise, you are wonderful, and I love you.
This is one of the best days of your life.
Everything is working out for your highest good.
Whatever you need to know is revealed to you.
Whatever you need comes to you.
All is well.

APRIL 8

I Do My Best to Help Create a Loving, Harmonious World

No soul has ever been harmed and therefore does not need redemption. It is our personalities that need to be reminded that we are spiritual beings having a human experience, not the other way around.

As we grow spiritually, we see the perfection of all of Life. The Universe waits in smiling repose for us to learn that loving unconditionally is the best way to live and will bring us peace, power, and riches beyond our current imagination. Affirm: *I do my best to help create a loving, harmonious world.*

I Am Lovable and Life Loves Me

Do this meditation sitting in front of a mirror. Place your hands over your heart. Take a deep breath. See yourself through the eyes of love. And speak to yourself with love.

> *I am lovable and Life loves me.*
> *I forgive myself for all the times*
> *I've been afraid I am not lovable.*
> *I am lovable and Life loves me.*
>
> *I forgive myself for judging myself and*
> *for not believing in my goodness.*
> *I am lovable and Life loves me.*
>
> *I forgive myself for feeling unworthy and*
> *for believing I don't deserve love.*
> *I am lovable and Life loves me.*
> *I forgive myself for all the times*
> *I've criticized and attacked myself.*
> *I am lovable and Life loves me.*
>
> *I forgive myself for my mistakes.*
> *I ask for forgiveness so that I can learn.*
> *I accept forgiveness so that I can grow.*
> *I am lovable and Life loves me.*

I OPEN MY HEART AND LET THE LOVE DISSOLVE THE FEAR

At any moment, I have the opportunity of choosing love or fear. In moments of fear, I remember the sun. It is always shining, even though clouds may obscure it for a while. Like the sun, the One Infinite Power is eternally shining its Light upon me, even though clouds of negative thinking may temporarily obscure it. I choose to remember the Light. I feel secure in the Light. And when the fears come, I choose to see them as passing clouds in the sky, and I let them go on their way. I am not my fears. It is safe for me to live without guarding and defending myself all the time. When I feel afraid, I open my heart and let the love dissolve the fear.

When One Door Closes, Another Door Opens

Life is a series of doors closing and opening. We walk from room to room having different experiences. Many of us would like to close some doors on old negative patterns, old blocks, and things that are no longer nourishing or useful for us. Many of us are in the process of opening new doors and finding wonderful new experiences—sometimes learning experiences and sometimes joyous experiences.

It is all part of Life, and we need to know that we really are safe. It is only change. From the very first door that we open when we come to this planet to the very last door that we open when we leave, we are always safe. It is only change. We are at peace with our own inner selves. We are safe and secure and loved.

I Express All My Feelings in Honest and Positive Ways

Anger is a natural and normal emotion. Babies get furious, express their fury, and then it's over. Many of us have learned that it's not nice, polite, or acceptable to be angry. We learn to swallow our angry feelings. They settle in our bodies, in the joints and muscles, and then they accumulate and become resentment. Layer upon layer of buried anger turned into resentment can contribute to dis-eases such as arthritis, assorted aches and pains, and even cancer.

We need to acknowledge all our emotions, including anger, and find positive ways to express these feelings. We don't have to hit people or dump on them, yet we can say simply and clearly, "This makes me angry," or "I'm angry about what you did." If it's not appropriate to say this, we still have many options: we can scream into a pillow, hit a punching bag, run, yell in the car with the windows rolled up, play tennis, or any number of other things. These are all healthy outlets.

I Am Willing to Learn What Life Is Trying to Teach Me

We want to be grateful for the lessons we have. Don't run from lessons; they are little packages of treasure that have been given to us. As we learn from them, our lives change for the better.

I now rejoice whenever I see another portion of the dark side of myself. I know that it means that I am ready to let go of something that has been hindering my life. I say, "Thank you for showing me this, so I can heal it and move on." So, whether the lesson is a "problem" that has cropped up, or an opportunity to see an old, negative pattern within us that it is time to let go of, rejoice!

I Free Myself from All Destructive Fears and Doubts

Fear is a limitation of our minds. People have so much fear about getting sick or about becoming homeless or whatever. Anger is fear that becomes a defense mechanism. It protects us, yet it would be so much more powerful to stop re-creating fearful situations in our minds and love ourselves through the fear. We are at the center of everything that happens in our lives. Every experience, every relationship, is the mirror of a mental pattern that we have inside us.

Affirmations for Releasing Fears

I am willing to release my fears.
I live and move in a safe and secure world.
I free myself from all destructive fears and doubts.
I accept myself and create peace in my mind and heart.
I rise above thoughts that attempt
to make me angry or afraid.
I release the past with ease and trust the process of life.
I am willing to release the need for this protection.
I am now willing to see only my magnificence.
I have the power to make changes.
I am always Divinely protected.

I JOYOUSLY RUN FORWARD TO GREET LIFE'S WONDERFUL EXPERIENCES

In order to be whole, we must accept all of ourselves. So let your heart open, and make plenty of room in there for all parts of yourself: the parts you are proud of, the parts that embarrass you, the parts you reject, and the parts you love. They are all you. You're beautiful. We all are. When your heart is full of love for yourself, then you have so much to share with others.

Let this love now fill your room and radiate out to all the people you know. Mentally put the people you care about in the center of your room, so that they can receive the love from your overflowing heart.

Now see the child in each of these people dancing as children dance, skipping and shouting and turning somersaults and cartwheels, filled with exuberant joy, expressing all the best of the child within. And let your inner child go and play with the other children. Let your child dance. Let your child feel safe and free. Let your child be all that it ever wanted to be.

You are perfect, whole, and complete, and all is well in your wonderful world. And so it is.

MY LIFE IS JUST
BEGINNING, AND I LOVE IT!

"What exactly is an affirmation?" Robert Holden asks.

"An affirmation is a new beginning," Louise replies.

Louise transformed her life by using affirmations. "I learned that every thought you think and every word you say is an affirmation," she says. "They affirm what you believe to be true and, therefore, how you experience your life." A complaint is an affirmation. Gratitude is an affirmation. Every thought and every word affirms something. Decisions and actions are also affirmations. The clothes you choose to wear, the foods you choose to eat, and the exercise you choose to do or not do—they are affirming your life.

The moment you say affirmations, you are stepping out of the victim role. You are no longer helpless. You are acknowledging your own power. Affirmations wake you up from the sleep of the daily unconscious. They help you choose your thoughts. They help you let go of old limiting beliefs. They help you to be more present. They help you to heal your future. "What you affirm today sets up a new experience of tomorrow," says Louise.

I Forgive All Perceived Wrongs and Release Them with Love

Many of us carry grudges for years and years. We feel self-righteous because of what *they* did to us. I call this being stuck in the prison of self-righteous resentment. We get to be right. We never get to be happy.

I can hear you saying, "But you don't know what they did to me; it's unforgivable." Being unwilling to forgive is a terrible thing to do to ourselves. Bitterness is like swallowing a teaspoon of poison every day. It accumulates and harms us. It is impossible to be healthy and free when we keep ourselves bound to the past.

The incident is over. Perhaps long over. Let it go. Allow yourself to be free. Come out of prison and step into the sunshine of life. If the incident is still going on, then ask yourself why you think so little of yourself that you still put up with it. Why do you stay in such a situation? Don't waste time trying to "get even." It doesn't work. What we give out always comes back to us. So let's drop the past and work on loving ourselves in the now. Then we shall have a wonderful future.

LOVING MYSELF IS MY MAGIC WAND

Every day it gets easier to look into my own eyes in the mirror and say, "I love you just the way you are." My life improves without me fixing it up. I used to be a fix-it person. I'd fix my relationships. I'd fix my bank account. I'd fix things with my boss, my health, and my creativity. Then one day I discovered magic. If I could really love myself, really love every part of me, incredible miracles happened in my life. My problems seemed to dissolve, and there was nothing to fix. So the focus of my attention has changed from fixing problems to loving myself and trusting the Universe to bring to me everything that I need and everything that I desire.

I Am Aware That I Can Never Lose Anyone and That I Am Never Lost

Death and Grief Treatment

I am at peace with the process of death and grieving. I give myself time and space to go through this natural, normal process of life. I am gentle with myself. I allow myself to work through the grief. I am aware that I can never lose anyone and that I am never lost. In the twinkling of an eye, I will connect with that soul again. Everyone dies. Trees, animals, birds, rivers, and even stars are born and die. And so do I. And all in the perfect time-space sequence.

I OPEN NEW DOORS TO LIFE

We have been going through doors since the moment we were born. That was a big door and a big change, and we have been through many doors since then.

We came to this lifetime equipped with everything we need in order to live fully and richly. We have all the wisdom and knowledge we need. We have all the abilities and talents we need. We have all the love we need. Life is here to support us and take care of us. We need to know and trust that this is so.

Doors are constantly closing and opening, and if we stay centered in ourselves, then we will always be safe, no matter which doorway we pass through. Even when we pass through the last doorway on this planet, it is not the end. It is simply the beginning of another new adventure. Trust that it is all right to experience change.

Today is a new day. We will have many wonderful new experiences. We are loved. We are safe.

The Universe Says Yes to Me

Receiving is a great big yes. "The Universe says yes to you," says Louise. "It wants you to experience your highest good. When you ask for your highest good, the Universe doesn't say, 'I'll think about it'; it says yes. The Universe is always saying yes to your highest good." And you have to say yes, too. The key to receiving is willingness, or readiness. When you declare, "I am ready to receive my highest good in this situation," it shifts your perception and your circumstances.

Receiving helps you to be present. It helps you to be where you are, to inhale deeply, and to take in everything that is here for you. "Often what's missing in a situation is only our ability to receive," says Louise. "The Universe always provides, but we have to be open and receptive to see this." The willingness to receive opens you up inside and takes you beyond your theories of what you believe you deserve and what you think is possible. Receiving helps you to pay attention to what is already here for you.

I Breathe in the Fullness and Richness of Life

You are meant to be a wonderful, loving expression of Life. Life is waiting for you to open up to it—to feel worthy of the good it holds for you. The wisdom and intelligence of the Universe is yours to use. Life is here to support you. Trust the Power within you to be there for you.

If you get scared, it is helpful to become aware of your breath as it flows in and out of your body. Your breath, the most precious substance of your life, is freely given to you. You have enough to last for as long as you live. You accept this precious substance without even thinking, and yet you doubt that life can supply you with the other necessities. Now is the time for you to learn about your own power and what you are capable of doing. Go within and find out who you are.

I LOVE MYSELF PERFECTLY AS I AM

We don't have to be "perfect parents." If we are loving parents, our children will have an excellent chance of growing up to be the kind of people we would like to have as friends. They will be individuals who are self-fulfilled and successful. Self-fulfillment brings inner peace. I think the best thing we can do for our children is to learn to love ourselves, for children always learn by example. We will have a better life, and they will have a better life.

I RADIATE SUCCESS, AND I PROSPER WHEREVER I TURN

Give up the mental struggle inside of you. Begin to allow yourself to totally enjoy your life as it is today. Be grateful and thankful for your creative talents. The Universe loves gratitude. Rejoice in the success of others. Make everything you do fun and creative. Love yourself and love your life. You are now moving to the next level. All is well. Affirm: *I radiate success, and I prosper wherever I turn.*

I AM WILLING TO LEARN
NEW THINGS EVERY DAY

If you feel resistant to change, look in the mirror and affirm:

It is only a thought, and a thought can be changed.
I am open to change.
I am willing to change.
I greet the new with open arms.
I am willing to learn new things every day.
Each problem has a solution.
All experiences are opportunities for me to learn and grow.
I am safe.

EVERY THOUGHT I THINK IS CREATING MY FUTURE

In Louise's live lecture *The Totality of Possibilities*, she says, "I spend my life seeing the truth in people. I see the absolute truth of their being. I know that the health of God is in them and can express itself through them." Louise isn't talking about positive thinking. In fact, Louise doesn't see thoughts as being positive or negative. Thoughts are always neutral. It's the way we handle our thoughts that is either positive or negative.

"So how do we really change our mind?" Robert Holden asks Louise.

"You have to change your relationship to your mind," she says.

"How do we do that?"

"By remembering that you are the thinker of your thoughts."

"Be the thinker, not the thought," he says.

"The power is with the thinker, not the thought," she responds.

My Life Is Whole and Complete, and I Am Ready for New Adventures!

Each moment of your life is perfect, whole, and complete. With God, nothing is ever unfinished. You are one with Infinite Power, Infinite Wisdom, Infinite Action, and Infinite Oneness. You wake up with a sense of fulfillment, knowing that you shall complete all that you undertake today. Each breath is full and comes to completion. Each scene you see is complete in itself. Each word you speak is full and complete. Each task you undertake, or each portion of that task, is completed to your satisfaction. You do not struggle alone in the wilderness of life. You release all belief in struggle and resistance.

You accept assistance from your many unseen friends who are always ready to lead you and guide you as you allow them to help. Everything in your life falls into place easily and effortlessly. Calls are completed on time. Letters are received and answered. Projects come to fruition. Others cooperate. Everything is on time and in perfect Divine right order. All is complete, and you feel good. This is a day of completion. Declare that it is so.

WE ARE HERE TO LOVE OURSELVES AND TO LOVE ONE ANOTHER

We are the only ones who can save the world. As we band together for the common cause, we find the answers. We must always remember that there is a part of us that is far more than our bodies, far more than our personalities, far more than our dis-eases, and far more than our past. There is a part of us that is more than our relationships. The very core of us is pure Spirit, eternal. It always has been and always will be. We are here to love ourselves and to love one another. By doing this, we will find the answers so that we can heal ourselves and the planet.

We are going through extraordinary times. All sorts of things are changing. We may not even know the depth of the problems, yet we are swimming as best we can. This, too, shall pass, and we will find solutions. We connect on a spiritual level, and on the level of Spirit, we are all one. We are free. And so it is.

I ALWAYS HAVE THE FREEDOM TO CHOOSE MY THOUGHTS

No person, place, or thing has any power over me unless I give it, for I am the only thinker in my mind. I have immense freedom in that I can choose what to think. I can choose to see life in positive ways instead of complaining or being mad at myself or other people. Complaining about what I don't have is one way to handle a situation, but it doesn't change anything. When I love myself and I find myself in the midst of a negative situation, I can say something like, "I'm willing to release the pattern in my consciousness that contributed to this condition."

We've all made negative choices in the past. Yet this does not mean we are bad people, nor are we stuck with these negative choices. We can always choose to let go of the old judgments.

I HONOR MY INNER CHILD BY REMEMBERING TO PLAY AND HAVE FUN

In order for a child to grow and blossom, he or she needs love, acceptance, and praise. We can be shown "better" ways to do things without making the way we do it "wrong." The child within you still needs that love and approval.

You can say the following positive statements to your inner child:

I love you and know that you're doing the best you can.
You're perfect just as you are.
You become more wonderful every day.
I approve of you.
Let's see if we can find a better way to do this.
Growing and changing is fun, and we can do it together.

I Will Always Be Perfect, Whole, and Complete

In the infinity of life where I am,
all is perfect, whole, and complete.
I no longer choose to believe in old limitations and lack.
I now choose to begin to see myself as the
Universe sees me—perfect, whole, and complete.
The truth of my Being is that I was
created perfect, whole, and complete.
I will always be perfect, whole, and complete.
I now choose to live my life from this understanding.
I am in the right place at the right time, doing the right thing.
All is well in my world.

I Am Willing to Let Life Love Me Today

Put this book down for a moment and repeat 10 times the affirmation *Life loves you*. Afterward, look in the mirror and say this affirmation to yourself: *I am willing to let Life love me today.* Notice your responses. And remember to breathe. Repeat this affirmation until you feel comfortable sensations in your body, light feelings in your heart, and a happy commentary in your thoughts. Willingness is the key. With willingness, all things are possible.

"I encourage people to be very kind to themselves when they do this practice," Louise says. "I know that mirror work can be very confronting at first. It reveals your most basic fear and your most terrible self-judgments. But if you keep looking in the mirror, you will begin to see through those judgments and see who you really are. Your attitude to mirror work is the key to success. It's important to take it lightly and be playful. If it helps, I prefer that people stop calling it mirror *work* and instead call it mirror *play*."

I Have the Power to Change My Life

Remember that whatever position you may find yourself in, your thinking got you there. The people around you are only mirroring what you believe you deserve.

Thoughts can be changed. Situations can be changed as well. That boss that we find intolerable could become our champion. That dead-end position with no hope of advancement may open up to a new career full of possibilities. The co-worker who is so annoying might turn out to be, if not a friend, at least someone who is easier to get along with. The salary that we find insufficient can increase in the twinkle of an eye. We could find a wonderful new job.

There are an infinite number of channels if we can change our thinking. Let's open ourselves up to them. We must accept in consciousness that abundance and fulfillment can come from anywhere. The change may be small at first, such as an added assignment from your boss in which you could demonstrate your intelligence and creativity. You may treat a co-worker as if they were not the enemy and, as a result, experience a notable change in behavior. Whatever the change may be, accept and rejoice in it. You are not alone. You are the change. The Power that created you has given you the power to create your own experiences!

I Am Willing to Change and Grow

Relationships are mirrors of ourselves. What we attract always mirrors either qualities we have or beliefs we have about relationships. This is true whether it is a boss, a co-worker, an employee, a friend, a lover, a spouse, or a child. The things you don't like about these people are either what you yourself do or would not do, or what you believe. You could not attract them or have them in your life if the way they are didn't somehow complement your own life.

Exercise: Us Versus Them

Look for a moment at someone in your life who bothers you. Describe three things about this person that you don't like, things that you want him or her to change.

Now, look deeply inside of you and ask yourself, "Where am I like that, and when do I do the same things?"

Close your eyes and give yourself the time to do this.

Then ask yourself if you *are willing to change*. When you remove these patterns, habits, and beliefs from your thinking and behavior, either the other person will change or he or she will leave your life.

I RELEASE THE WORD *SHOULD* AND SET MYSELF FREE

As I've said many times, I believe that *should* is one of the most damaging words in our language. Every time we use it, we are, in effect, saying that we *are* wrong, or we *were* wrong, or we're *going to be* wrong. I would like to take the word *should* out of our vocabulary forever, and replace it with the word *could*. This word gives us a choice, and then we're never wrong.

Think of five things that you "should" do. Then replace *should* with *could*.

Now, ask yourself, "Why haven't I?" You may find that you've been berating yourself for years for something that you never wanted to do in the first place, or for something that was never your idea. How many "shoulds" can you drop from your list?

MY BODY IS A GOOD FRIEND
THAT I TAKE LOVING CARE OF

Louise says, "I always thank my stove for working well when I cook." So when *you* are in the kitchen, get in the habit of thanking your appliances. Thank your dishwasher, the blender, your teapot, the refrigerator, and so on, and use these affirmations while there:

Hello, kitchen, you are my
nourishment center. I appreciate you!
You and all your appliances help me so much in
easily preparing delicious, nutritious meals.
There is such an abundance of
good, healthy food in my fridge.
I can easily make a delicious, nutritious meal.
You help me be cheerful.
I love you.

I FEED MY BODY WITH FOOD
THAT LOVES MY BODY

Everything is thoughts and food. If you have good nutrition, it serves your brain. If you start to shift and change the food you eat, then it's easier to grasp on to new, positive thoughts and make better choices in your life.

Start with this affirmation: *I love myself, therefore, I lovingly feed my body nourishing foods and beverages and my body lovingly responds with vibrant health and energy.*

I Am Willing to Love and Accept My Inner Child

It doesn't matter how old you are; there is a little child within you who needs love and acceptance. If you are a woman, no matter how self-reliant you are, you have a little girl inside who is very tender and needs help. If you are a man, no matter how self-confident you are, you have a little boy inside of you who craves warmth and affection.

Every time you feel scared, realize that it is the child within you who is scared. The adult isn't afraid, yet it has disconnected and isn't there for the child. The adult and the child need to develop a relationship with each other.

All your inner child really wants is to be noticed, to feel safe, and to be loved. If you can take just a few moments a day to begin to connect with the little person inside of you, life is going to be a lot better.

Let's affirm: *I am willing to love and accept my inner child.*

I Make a Vow to Treat Myself with Loving-Kindness

We all have areas of our lives that we think are unacceptable and unlovable. If we are really angry with parts of ourselves, we often engage in self-abuse. We abuse alcohol, drugs, or cigarettes; we overeat, or whatever. We beat ourselves up. One of the worst things we do, which does more damage than anything else, is criticize ourselves. We need to stop all criticism. Once we get into the practice of doing that, it is amazing how we stop criticizing other people—because everyone is a reflection of us, and what we see in another person we see in ourselves.

When we complain about another person, we are really complaining about ourselves. When we can truly love and accept who we are, there is nothing to complain about. We cannot hurt ourselves and we cannot hurt another person. Let's make a vow that we will no longer criticize ourselves for anything.

I REMEMBER TO HAVE FUN TODAY

There is no need to make drudgery out of what you are doing. It can be fun. It can be a game. It can be a joy. It's up to you! Even practicing forgiveness and releasing resentment can be fun, if you want to make it so. Again, make up a little song about that person or situation that is so hard to release. When you sing a ditty, it lightens up the whole procedure. When I work with clients privately, I bring laughter into the procedure as soon as I can. The quicker we can laugh about the whole thing, the easier it is to let it go.

If you saw your problems on a stage in a play by Neil Simon, you would laugh yourself right out of the chair. Tragedy and comedy are the same thing. It just depends on your viewpoint! Oh, "what fools we mortals be."

Do whatever you can to make your transformational change a joy and a pleasure. Have fun!

HOW MIGHT I HELP?

There are a lot of people who need goals in life— a one-year goal or a five-year goal—but that was never me. I wasn't really trying to do anything that was well defined or narrowly focused. My question was always: *How can I help people?* I have asked that question thousands of times, and I continue to ask it today. When I see all the difficult things that are happening in the world, I realize that I might not be able to do anything specific, but what I *can* do is ask the question and project the intention energetically of *How might I help?*

My Goal Is to Be in Love with Every *Now* Moment

I put love into my daily schedule, whether I go to the market or the office or travel around the world or just stay at home. One of our purposes in life is to help heal the world. So we start with healing ourselves. The center of our world is wherever we are. Our thoughts go out from us like ripples in a pond. When we create harmony inside by thinking harmonious thoughts, then that energy goes out from us into the world, touching people and places and things. These vibrations are felt and responded to. Let's make sure that we are radiating harmony and love.

I Am Very Thankful for All the Love in My Life

Love comes when we least expect it, when we are not looking for it. Hunting for love never brings the right partner. It only creates longing and unhappiness. Love is never outside ourselves; love is within us.

Don't insist that love come immediately. Perhaps you are not ready for it, or you are not developed enough to attract the love you want. Don't settle for anybody just to have someone. Set your standards. What kind of love do you want to attract? List the qualities in yourself, and you will attract a person who has them. You might examine what may be keeping love away. Could it be criticism? Feelings of unworthiness? Unreasonable standards? Movie star images? Fear of intimacy? A belief that you are unlovable?

Be ready for love when it does come. Prepare the field and be ready to nourish love. Be loving, and you will be lovable. Be open and receptive to love.

I Do Work I Love, and I Am Well Paid for It

Affirmations for Career Growth

*I get along with all my co-workers in
an atmosphere of mutual respect.
I work for people who respect me and pay me well.
My work space is a pleasure to be in.
It is easy for me to find employment.
My income is constantly increasing.
My work is fulfilling and satisfying.
I always have wonderful bosses.
It is a pleasure to come to work.
I have a great work life.
I appreciate my career.*

Every Cell in My Body Has Divine Intelligence

In the infinity of life where I am,
all is perfect, whole, and complete.
I recognize my body as a good friend.
Each cell in my body has Divine Intelligence.
I listen to what it tells me and know that its advice is valid.
I am always safe and Divinely protected and guided.
I choose to be healthy and free.
All is well in my world.

TODAY I ASK LOVE TO TEACH ME TO LOVE

Loving communication is one of the happiest and most powerful experiences for people. How do I get to this space? I have done a lot of work on myself, I've read many books, and I've come to understand the principles of life, such as, "What I think and say goes out from me, the Universe responds, and it comes back to me." So I begin to ask for help and to observe myself. As I allow myself the space to watch without judgment and without criticism, I begin to make great progress in loving communication. What do I believe? What do I feel? How do I react? How can I love more? And then I say to the Universe, "Teach me to love."

I ACCEPT HEALING AND GOOD HEALTH HERE AND NOW

Good health is my Divine right. I am open and receptive to all the healing energies in the Universe. I know that every cell in my body is intelligent and knows how to heal itself. My body is always working toward perfect health. I now release any and all impediments to my perfect healing. I learn about nutrition and feed my body only wholesome food. I watch my thinking and think only healthy thoughts. I love my body. I send love to each organ, bone, muscle, and part of my body. I flood the cells of my body with love. I am grateful to my body for all the good health I have had in the past. I accept healing and good health here and now.

When I Fix My Thinking, It Fixes My Problems

If you are in a job you don't care for, if you want to change your position, if you are having problems at work, or if you are out of work, the best way to handle it is this:

Begin by blessing your current position with love. Realize that this is only a stepping-stone on your pathway. You are where you are because of your own thinking patterns. If "they" are not treating you the way you would like to be treated, then there is a pattern in your consciousness that is attracting such behavior. So, in your mind, look around your current job or the job you had last, and begin to bless everything with love—the building, the elevators or stairs, the rooms, the furniture and equipment, the people you work for and the people you work with—and each and every customer.

Begin to affirm for yourself: *I always work for the most wonderful bosses. My boss always treats me with respect and courtesy. My boss is generous and easy to work for.* This will carry forward with you all your life, and if you become a boss, then you will be like that, too.

MY FORGIVING ATTITUDE ATTRACTS FRESH INSPIRATION AND NEW BEGINNINGS

You can never be free of bitterness as long as you continue to think unforgiving thoughts. How can you be happy in this moment if you continue to choose to be angry and resentful? Thoughts of bitterness can't create joy. No matter how justified you feel you are, no matter what "they" did, if you insist on holding on to the past, then you will never be free. Forgiving yourself and others will release you from the prison of the past.

When you feel that you're stuck in some situation, or when your affirmations aren't working, it usually means that there's more forgiveness work to be done. When you don't flow freely with life in the present moment, it usually means that you're holding on to a past moment. It can be regret, sadness, hurt, fear, guilt, blame, anger, resentment, or sometimes even a desire for revenge. Each one of these states comes from a space of unforgiveness, a refusal to let go and come into the present moment. Only in the present moment can you create your future.

I AM ALWAYS SAFE
AND DIVINELY PROTECTED

I am one with Life, and all of Life loves and supports me. Therefore, I claim for myself love and acceptance on all levels. I accept all of my emotions and can express them appropriately when the occasion arises. I am not my parents, nor am I attached to their patterns of anger and judgment. I have learned to observe rather than react, and now life is much less tumultuous. I am my own unique self, and I no longer choose to sweat the small stuff. I have peace of mind. This is the truth of my being, and I accept it as so. All is well in my inner being.

I Am a Unique Expression of the Eternal Oneness

I am here to learn to love myself and to love other people unconditionally. Even though every person has measurable things about them, such as height and weight, there is far more to me than my physical expression. The immeasurable part of me is where my power is. Comparing myself with others makes me feel either superior or inferior, never acceptable exactly as I am. What a waste of time and energy. We are all unique, wonderful beings, each different and special. I go within and connect with the unique expression of eternal oneness that I am and we all are.

I GREET MY INNER CHILD WITH LOVE

Walk over to your mirror. Look deeply into your eyes. Look beyond the adult you see in your mirror and greet your inner child. What is this child trying to tell you?

1. Find a photo of yourself when you were about five years old. Tape the photo to your bathroom mirror.

2. Look at the photo for a few minutes. What do you see? Do you see a happy child? A miserable child?

3. Talk to your inner child in the mirror. You can look at the photo or even look into your own eyes—whichever feels more comfortable for you. If you had a nickname as a child, use this name as you speak to your inner child. What works really well is to sit in front of the mirror, because if you are standing, as soon as difficult feelings start to come up, you might be tempted to run out the door. So sit down, grab a box of tissues, and start talking.

4. Open your heart and share your innermost thoughts.

5. When you are finished, say these affirmations: *I love you, dear one. I am here for you. You are safe.*

FORGIVENESS HELPS ME
CREATE A BETTER FUTURE

Forgiveness is a tricky and confusing concept for many people, but know that there's a difference between forgiveness and acceptance. Forgiving someone doesn't mean that you condone their behavior! The act of forgiveness takes place in your own mind. It really has nothing to do with the other person. The reality of true forgiveness lies in setting yourself free from the pain.

Also, forgiveness doesn't mean allowing the painful behaviors or actions of another to continue in your life. Taking a stand and setting healthy boundaries is often the most loving thing you can do—not only for yourself, but for the other person as well.

No matter what your reasons are for having bitter, unforgiving feelings, you can go beyond them. You have a choice. You can choose to stay stuck and resentful, or you can do yourself a favor by willingly forgiving what happened in the past; letting it go; and then moving on to create a joyous, fulfilling life. You have the freedom to make your life anything you want it to be because you have freedom of choice.

I CHOOSE MY OWN
LOVING CONCEPT OF GOD

I have the power to choose to see things as they really are. I choose to see things as God does, with the eyes of love. Since it is the nature of God to be present everywhere, to be all-powerful and all-knowing, I know that all there really is in this entire Universe is the love of God. The love of God surrounds me, indwells me, goes before me, and smooths the way for me. I am a beloved child of the Universe, and the Universe lovingly takes care of me now and forevermore. When I need something, I turn to the Power that created me. I ask for what I need, and then I give thanks even before receiving, knowing that it will come to me in the perfect time-space sequence.

EVERY CHOICE I MAKE
IS PERFECT FOR ME

What brings you joy? What makes your heart sing? Go within and trust the process of life to reveal your true purpose to you. You will find that in doing what you truly love, the money will follow, the weight will stabilize, and the digestion problems will subside. In the meantime, find something that really makes you happy, and pursue it. Bless the path you have been on, and know that it was perfect for you at that particular time.

Now it is time to open your arms to the Universe and lovingly embrace yourself as you begin this new unfolding of Divine order in your life. A wonderful affirmation for you is: *I trust the process of life. Every choice I make is the perfect choice for me. I am safe; it's only change. I lovingly release the past, and I now create a new and wonderful career that is deeply fulfilling for me. And so it is!*

I BLESS MY JOB WITH LOVE

A young man was about to start a new job and was nervous. I remember saying, "Why wouldn't you do well? *Of course* you will be successful. Open your heart and let your talents flow out of you. Bless the establishment, all of the people you work with, and the people you work for, and each and every customer with love, and all will go well."

He did just that and was a great success.

If you want to leave your job, then begin to affirm that you release your current job with love to the next person who will be delighted to have it. Know that there are people out there looking for exactly what you have to offer, and that you are being brought together on the checkerboard of life even now.

I Love My Car

Driving is a safe and pleasant experience for me. I take good care of my car, and my car takes good care of me. It is ready to go whenever I am. I have the perfect mechanic, who also loves my car. I fill my car with love whenever I enter it, so love is always traveling with me. I send love to other drivers on the road, as we are all traveling together. Love goes before me, and love greets me at my destination.

I HAVE THE POWER TO CHANGE
MY THOUGHTS—AND THE WORLD

If each one of us would practice getting in touch with the treasures within us on a daily basis, we could literally change the world. People living the truth change the world. For the truth of our being is that we are filled with unconditional love. We are filled with incredible joy. We are filled with serene peace. We are connected to Infinite Wisdom. What we need to do is to know it and live it!

Today we are mentally preparing for tomorrow. The thoughts we think, the words we speak, the beliefs we accept, shape our tomorrows. Every morning, stand in front of a mirror and affirm to yourself:

I am filled with unconditional love, and I express it today.
I am filled with joy, and I express it today.
I am filled with peace, and I share it today.
I am filled with Infinite Wisdom, and I practice it today.
And this is the truth about me.

I Love Being Me

I see myself having a consciousness of oneness with the presence and power of God. I see myself ever aware of the power of God within me as the source of everything I desire. I see myself confidently calling upon the Presence to supply my every need. I love all expressions of God unconditionally, knowing the truth of all that is. I walk through life with the happy companionship of my Godself, and joyfully express the goodness that I am. My wisdom and understanding of Spirit increases, and I express more fully each day the inner beauty and strength of my true being.

Divine order is ever present in my experience, and there is plenty of time for all that I choose to do. I express wisdom, understanding, and love in all my dealings with others; and my words are Divinely guided. I see myself expressing the creative energy of Spirit in my work, writing and speaking words of truth easily and with a depth of understanding and wisdom. Fun, uplifting ideas flow through my consciousness for joyful expression, and I follow through on the ideas received, bringing them into full manifestation.

AS I SAY YES TO LIFE, LIFE SAYS YES TO ME

"All I've ever done is listen to my inner ding and said yes," Louise says, as she reflects on her career as a writer and teacher. "I never meant to write a book. My first book, the little blue book *Heal Your Body*, was just a list I compiled. Someone suggested I make it into a book. And I said yes. I had no idea how to publish a book, but helping hands appeared along the way. It was just a little adventure." Little did she realize that her "little adventure" would be a bestseller and the catalyst for a self-help revolution in publishing.

Louise's story about giving talks follows a similar pattern. "Someone invited me to give a talk and I said yes. I had no idea what I'd say, but as soon as I said yes I felt guided along the way." First came talks, then workshops, and then the Hayrides. "A few gay men regularly attended my workshops," Louise recalls. "Then one day I was asked if I'd be willing to start a group for people with AIDS. I said, 'Yes, let's get together and see what happens.'" There wasn't a grand marketing plan. She didn't target appearing on *The Oprah Winfrey Show* and *The Phil Donahue Show*. "I followed my heart," says Louise.

LOVING OTHERS IS EASY WHEN
I LOVE AND ACCEPT MYSELF

Affirmations for Strengthening Friendships

*I am willing to release the pattern in me
that attracts troubled friendships.*
I love and accept myself, and I am a magnet for friends.
All my friendships are successful.
I am a loving and nurturing friend.
I trust myself, I trust Life, and I trust my friends.
Loving others is easy when I love and accept myself.
Even if I make a mistake, my friends help me through.
I deserve to be supported.
My friends are loving and supportive.
My friends and I have total freedom to be ourselves.
My love and acceptance of others creates lasting friendships.

I Am Teachable, I Can Learn, I Am Willing to Change

*In the infinity of life where I am,
all is perfect, whole, and complete.
I now choose calmly and objectively to see my
old patterns, and I am willing to make changes.
I am teachable. I can learn. I am willing to change.
I choose to have fun doing this.
I choose to react as though I have found a treasure
when I discover something else to release.
I see and feel myself changing moment by moment.
Thoughts no longer have any power over me.
I am the power in the world. I choose to be free.
All is well in my world.*

I More I Love Myself, the More I Feel Loved by Life

"Life is always trying to love us, but we need to be open if we are to see it," Louise tells Robert Holden.

"How do we stay open?" he asks.

"By being willing to love yourself," she says.

"Loving yourself is the key to letting life love you."

"When you project your lack of self-love onto others, you accuse them of not loving you enough, and all you see is an unfriendly Universe," Louise explains.

"'Projection makes perception,'" he says, sharing a line from *A Course in Miracles*.

"Fear shows us one world; and love shows us another world," says Louise. "We decide which world is real. And we decide which world we want to live in."

Every Problem Has a Solution

There aren't any problems that don't have solutions. There aren't any questions without answers. Choose to go beyond the problem to seek the Divine solution to any type of discord that seems to appear. Be willing to learn from any strife or confusion as it comes up. It's important to release all blame and turn within to seek the truth. And be willing to release whatever pattern may be in your consciousness that has contributed to the situation.

I TRUST IN A HIGHER POWER TODAY

I learned a long time ago that I am a being of oneness with the presence and power of God, that the wisdom and understanding of Spirit resides within me, and I am, therefore, Divinely guided in all my dealings with others upon the planet. Just as all the stars and planets are in their perfect orbit, I am also in my Divine right order. I may not understand everything with my limited human mind; however, on the cosmic level, I know I am in the right place, at the right time, doing the right thing. My present experience is a stepping-stone to new awareness and new opportunities.

I DESERVE AND ACCEPT
MY SUCCESSFUL CAREER NOW

If you like your job but feel you are not getting paid enough, then begin to bless your current salary with love. Expressing gratitude for what we already have enables it to grow. Affirm that you are now opening your consciousness to a greater prosperity and that *part* of that prosperity is an increased salary. Affirm that you deserve a raise, not for negative reasons but because you are a great asset to the company and the owners want to share their profits with you. Always do the best you can on the job, for then the Universe will know that you are ready to be lifted out of where you are to the next and even better place.

Your consciousness put you where you are now. Your consciousness will either keep you there or lift you to a better position. It's up to you.

I BLESS MY INCOME WITH
LOVE AND WATCH IT GROW

My income is perfect for me. Every day I love myself a little more, and as I do, I find that I am open to new avenues of income. Prosperity comes through many forms and channels. It is not limited. Some people limit their incomes by saying that they live on a fixed income. But who fixed it? Some people feel that they don't deserve to earn more than their father earned or to go beyond their parents' worthiness level. Well, I can love my parents and still go beyond their income level. There is One Infinite Universe, and out of it comes all the income that everyone makes. The income I am presently making reflects my beliefs and my deservability. It has nothing to do with getting. It's really allowing myself to accept. I accept a healthy flow of income for myself.

I EXPERIENCE MIRACLES IN MY WORK EVERY DAY

Blessing with love is a powerful tool to use in any work environment. Send it ahead of you before you arrive. Bless every person, place, or thing there with love. If you have a problem, bless it with love. Affirm that you and the person or situation are in agreement and in perfect harmony.

*I am in perfect harmony with my
work environment and everyone in it.
I always work in harmonious surroundings.
I honor and respect each person,
and they, in turn, honor and respect me.
I bless this situation with love and know that
it works out the best for everyone concerned.
I bless you with love and release you to your highest good.
I bless this job and release it to someone who will love it, and
I am free to accept a wonderful new opportunity.*

Select or adapt one of these affirmations to fit a situation in your workplace, and repeat it over and over. Every time the person or situation comes into mind, repeat the affirmation. Eliminate the negative energy in your mind regarding this situation. You can, just by thinking, change the experience.

I Feel Safe in the Rhythm and Flow of Ever-Changing Life

When I used to work with clients privately, I would hear them argue on behalf of their limitations, and they would always want me to know why they were stuck because of one reason or another. If we believe we are stuck and accept that we are stuck, then we are stuck. We get "stuck" because our negative beliefs are being fulfilled. Instead, let's begin to focus on our strengths.

Many of you tell me that my tapes saved your lives. I want you to realize that no book or tape is going to save you. A little piece of tape in a plastic box is not saving your life. What you are doing with the information is what matters. I can give you plenty of ideas, yet what you do with them is going to count. I suggest that you listen to a particular tape over and over again for a month or more so that the ideas become a new habit pattern. I'm not your healer or savior. The only person who is going to make a change in your life is *you*.

IT IS ONLY A THOUGHT, AND A THOUGHT CAN BE CHANGED

All the events you have experienced in your lifetime up to this moment have been created by your thoughts and beliefs you have held in the past. They were created by the thoughts and words you used yesterday; last week; last month; last year; 10, 20, 30, 40, or more years ago, depending on how old you are.

However, that is your past. It is over and done with. What is important in this moment is what you are choosing to think and believe and say right now. For these thoughts and words will create your future. Your point of power is in the present moment and is forming the experience of tomorrow, next week, next month, next year, and so on.

You might notice what thought you are thinking at this moment. Is it negative or positive? Do you want this thought to be creating your future? Just notice and be aware.

TODAY I CREATE A
WONDERFUL NEW FUTURE

We are learning how Life works. It is like learning your computer. When you first get a computer, you learn the simple, basic processes—how to turn it on and off, how to open and save a document, how to print. And on that level, your computer works wonders for you. And yet, there is so much more that it can do for you when you learn more of its ways.

It is the same thing with Life. The more we learn how it works, the more wonders it performs for us.

There is a rhythm and flow to Life, and I am part of it. Life supports me and brings me only good and positive experiences. I trust the process of Life to bring me my highest good.

Every Day in Every Way I Am Feeling Healthier and Healthier

We all have ideas and habits around the food we eat and the thoughts we think about health. If you put yourself in the position where you know you can create healthy habits around food and trust that you can be healed, the right information and support will come to you. If you believe something is too hard, takes too much time, or can't be done, your life and habits will reflect that. When you shift to believing it can be done, the *how* will show up.

Affirm:

Hi, body, thank you for being so healthy.
My health is easy and effortless.
I am healed and whole.
I am worthy of being healed.
My body knows how to heal itself.
Every day and in every way I am
feeling healthier and healthier.
I love selecting foods that are nutritious and delicious.
My body loves the way I choose
the perfect foods for every meal.
Planning healthy meals is a joy. I am worth it.
When I feed myself healthy foods, I nourish
my body and mind for the day ahead.

I Choose to Feel Good about Myself Today

I think the real goal in life is to feel good. We want money because we want to feel better. We want good health because we want to feel better. We want a nice relationship because we think we will feel better. And if we could just make feeling better our goal, we would eliminate a lot of extra work. How can I really feel good in this moment? What thoughts can I think *right now* that will make me feel better? That's the question we need to constantly be asking ourselves.

MY UNIQUE CREATIVE TALENTS AND ABILITIES FLOW THROUGH ME

*In the infinity of life where I am,
all is perfect, whole, and complete.
My unique creative talents and abilities flow through
me and are expressed in deeply satisfying ways.
There are people out there who are always looking
for my services. I am always in demand and
can pick and choose what I want to do.
I earn good money doing what satisfies me.
My work is a joy and a pleasure.
All is well in my world.*

I Am Worth Loving

Affirmations for Embracing Sexuality

It is safe for me to explore my sexuality.
I express my desires with joy and freedom.
God created and approves of my sexuality.
I love myself and my sexuality.
I am safe and secure in my love for myself.
I give myself permission to enjoy my body.
I go beyond limiting beliefs and accept myself totally.
I am safe to be me in all situations.
My sexuality is a wonderful gift.
I am worth loving.

I Am in Charge of My Life Now

Many of us have an inner child who is lost and lonely and feels rejected. Perhaps the only contact we have had with our inner child for a long time is to scold and criticize it. Then we wonder why we are unhappy. We cannot reject a part of ourselves and still be in harmony within.

For now, visualize that you are taking your inner child by the hand and going everywhere together for a few days. See what joyous experiences you can have. This may sound silly, but please try it. It really works. Create a wonderful life for yourself and your inner child. The Universe will respond, and you will find ways to heal your inner child and the adult you.

Let's affirm: *I love my inner child. I am in charge of my life now.*

I Listen to the Wisdom of My Body

Pain comes to us in many forms: an ache, a scratch, a stubbed toe, a bruise, congestion, uneasy sleep, a queasy feeling in the stomach, a dis-ease. It is trying to tell us something. Pain is the body's way of waving a red flag to get our attention—a last-ditch effort to inform us that something is wrong in our life.

When we feel pain, what do we do? We usually run to the medicine cabinet or the drugstore and take a pill. When we do this, we are saying to our body, "Shut up! I don't want to hear you."

At some point, however, you have to pay attention to what's going on. Allow yourself to listen to your body, because fundamentally your body wants to be healthy, and it needs you to cooperate with it.

Think of every pain you have as a teacher, telling you that there's a false idea in your consciousness. Something you are believing, saying, doing, or thinking is not for your highest good. I always picture the body tugging at me, saying, "*Please* pay attention!" When you discover the mental pattern behind a pain or illness, you have a chance to change the pattern through your mirror work and arrest the dis-ease.

I LET GO OF BELIEFS THAT DON'T SUPPORT AND NURTURE ME

Loving and approving of yourself, trusting in the process of life, and feeling safe because you know the power of your own mind are extremely important issues when dealing with addictive behavior. My experiences with addicted persons have shown me that most share a deep self-hatred. They are very unforgiving of themselves. Day after day, they punish themselves. Why? Because somewhere along the line as children, they bought the idea that they were not good enough; they were bad and in need of punishment. Early childhood experiences that involve physical, emotional, or sexual abuse contribute to that self-hatred. Honesty, forgiveness, self-love, and a willingness to live in the truth can help to heal these early wounds and give the addictive person a reprieve from their behavior. I also find the addictive personality to be a fearful one. There is a great fear of letting go and trusting the life process. As long as we believe that the world is an unsafe place with people and situations waiting to "get" us—then that belief will be our reality.

Are you willing to let go of ideas and beliefs that don't support and nurture you? Then you are ready to continue our journey.

I RELEASE ALL NEGATIVE ADDICTIONS FROM MY LIFE

I am one with Life, and all of Life loves me and supports me. Therefore, I claim for myself high self-worth and self-esteem. I love and appreciate myself on every level. I am not my parents, nor any addictive pattern they may have had. No matter what my past may have been, now in this moment I choose to eliminate all negative self-talk and to love and approve of myself. I am my own unique self, and I rejoice in who I am. I am acceptable and lovable. This is the truth of my being, and I accept it as so. All is well in my world.

As I Forgive Myself, It Becomes Easier to Forgive Others

When the word *forgiveness* is mentioned, who comes to your mind? Who is the person or what is the experience that you feel you will never forget, never forgive? What is it that holds you to the past? When you refuse to forgive, you hold on to the past, and it is impossible for you to be in the present. It is only when you are in the present that you can create your future. Forgiving is a gift to yourself. It frees you from the past, the past experience, and past relationships. It allows you to live in present time. When you forgive yourself and forgive others, you are indeed free.

There is a tremendous sense of freedom that comes with forgiveness. Often you need to forgive yourself for putting up with painful experiences and not loving yourself enough to move away from those experiences. So love yourself, forgive yourself, forgive others, and be in the moment. See the old bitterness and the old pain just roll off your shoulders as you let the doors of your heart open wide. When you come from a space of love, you are always safe. Forgive everyone. Forgive yourself. Forgive all past experiences. You are free.

Everything I Need Comes to Me at the Perfect Time

I believe that everything I need to know is revealed to me, so I need to keep my eyes and ears open. When I had cancer, I remember thinking that a foot reflexologist would be very helpful for me. One evening I went to a lecture of some sort. Right after I sat down, a foot reflexologist sat next to me. We began to talk, and I learned that he even made house calls. I didn't have to look for him; he came to me.

I also believe that whatever I need comes to me in the perfect time-space sequence. When something goes wrong in my life, I immediately start to think, *All is well, it's okay, I know that this is all right. It's a lesson, an experience, and I'll pass through it. There is something here that is for my highest good. All is well. Just breathe. It's okay.* I do the best I can to calm myself, so I can think rationally about whatever is going on, and, of course, I do work through everything. It may take a little time, but sometimes, things that seem to be great disasters really turn out to be quite good in the end, or at least, not the disasters that they seemed to be in the beginning. Every event is a learning experience.

I Am Pure Spirit

I follow my inner star and sparkle and shine in my own unique way. I am a very precious being. I have a beautiful soul, and I have an outer body and a personality. But my soul is the center. My soul is the part of me that is eternal. It always has been and always will be. My soul has taken on many personalities. And will take on many more. My soul cannot be hurt or destroyed. It can only be enriched by whatever the life experiences are. There is so much more to life than I can comprehend. I shall never know all the answers. But the more I allow myself to understand how life works, the more of the power and force I have available to use.

I Take Care of My Inner Child Today

Take care of your inner child. It is the child who is frightened. It is the child who is hurting. It is the child who does not know what to do. Be there for your child. Embrace it and love it and do whatever you can to take care of its needs. Be sure to let your child know that no matter what happens, you will always be there for it. You will never turn away or desert it. You will always love this child.

I GLADLY RELEASE ALL
RESISTANCE TO LOVING MYSELF

Louise is asked about common mistakes people make doing mirror work. "Not doing mirror work is the biggest mistake!" Louise says. "Too many people don't do mirror work because they think it won't work before they've tried it." Once people start, they are often put off by the self-judging they witness, she says. "The flaws you see are not the truth of your being," Louise explains. "When you judge, you see flaws. When you love, you see your essence."

She is then asked about common blocks to doing mirror work. "Mirror work doesn't work in theory; it only works in practice," Louise says. In other words, the key to mirror work is to do it and to be consistent about it. When Louise is asked if she still has days when she finds it difficult to look in the mirror, she replies, "Yes, and on those days I make sure I stay in front of the mirror until I feel better." She doesn't go out the front door until she feels in a more loving space. After all, the world mirrors how we feel about ourselves.

JUNE 24

I LOVINGLY FORGIVE MYSELF

I love the feeling of freedom when I take off my heavy coat of criticism, fear, guilt, resentment, and shame. I can then forgive myself and others. This sets us all free. I am willing to give up my "stuff" around old issues. I refuse to live in the past any longer. I forgive myself for having carried those old burdens for so long. I forgive myself for not knowing how to love myself and others.

We are all responsible for our own behavior, and what we give out, life will give back to us. So I have no need to punish anyone. We are all under the laws of our own consciousness. I go about my own business of clearing out the unforgiving parts of my mind, and I allow the love to come in. Then, I am healed and whole.

THE MORE GRATEFUL I AM, THE MORE I GET TO BE GRATEFUL ABOUT

Gratitude brings more to be grateful about. It increases your abundant life. Lack of gratitude, or complaining, brings little to rejoice about. Complainers always find that they have little good in their life, or they do not enjoy what they do have. The Universe always gives us what we believe we deserve. Many of us have been raised to look at what we do not have and to feel only lack. We come from a belief in scarcity and then wonder why our lives are so empty. If we believe that "I don't have, and I won't be happy until I do . . ." then we are putting our lives on hold. What the Universe hears is: "I don't have, and I am not happy," and that is what you get more of.

For quite some time now, I've been accepting every compliment and every present with: "I accept with joy and pleasure and gratitude." I have learned that the Universe loves this expression, and I constantly get the most wonderful presents.

When I Meditate, I Balance My Body

When I meditate, I usually close my eyes, take a deep breath, and ask: *What is it I need to know?* I then sit and listen. I might also ask, *What is it I need to learn?* or *What is the lesson in this?* Sometimes, we think we're supposed to fix everything in our lives, but maybe we're really only supposed to learn something from the situation.

When I first began to meditate, I had violent headaches the first three weeks. Meditation was so unfamiliar and against all my usual inner programming. Nevertheless, I hung in there, and the headaches eventually disappeared.

If you are constantly coming up with a tremendous amount of negativity when you meditate, it may mean that it *needs* to come up, and when you quiet yourself, it starts to flow to the surface. Simply see the negativity being released. Try not to fight it. Allow it to continue as long as it needs to.

If you fall asleep when you meditate, that's all right. Let the body do what it needs to do; it will balance out in time.

I Give Myself Permission to Be Prosperous

There is an inexhaustible supply in the Universe. Begin to be aware of it. Take the time to count the stars on a clear evening, or the grains of sand in one handful, the leaves on one branch of a tree, the raindrops on a windowpane, the seeds in one tomato. Each seed is capable of producing a whole vine with unlimited tomatoes on it. Be grateful for what you do have, and you will find that it increases. I like to bless with love all that is in my life now: my home—the heat, water, light, telephone, furniture, plumbing, appliances—and clothing, transportation, jobs, the money I do have, friends, my ability to see and feel and taste and touch and walk and to enjoy this incredible planet.

Our own belief in lack and limitation is the only thing that is limiting us. What belief is limiting you?

I Say Yes to Being a Better Receiver

Receiving is the best psychotherapy. If you're really serious about receiving and you're willing to make it a daily practice, you'll find that receiving will help dissolve all your barriers to love. By declaring *I am willing to be a better receiver*, you activate a Power within you that can heal learned unworthiness, dysfunctional independence, unhealthy sacrifice, financial insecurity, and every type of lack. Receiving helps you to know your true worth and to live with ease and happiness.

I encourage you to start the spiritual practice of keeping a receiving journal. Spend 15 minutes a day, for the next seven days, cultivating an even greater willingness to receive. In your receiving journal, write down 10 responses to the sentence: *One way Life is loving me right now is* . . . Don't edit your responses. Just let them flow.

I Express My Love in All That I Do Today

I am one with Life, and all of Life loves and supports me. Therefore, I claim the best creative self-expression possible. My work environment is deeply fulfilling to me. I am loved, appreciated, and respected. I am not my parents, nor do I duplicate their own work-experience patterns. I am my own unique self, and I choose to do work that brings me even more satisfaction than the money. Work is now a joy for me. This is the truth of my being, and I accept it as so. All is well in my working world.

I MOVE BEYOND MY ADDICTIONS
AND SET MYSELF FREE

Affirmations for Addictions

*I see any resistance patterns within
me only as something to release.*

*I am loved and nourished
and supported by Life itself.*

*I am doing the best that I can.
Each day gets easier.*

*I am willing to release the
need for my addictions.*

*I move beyond my addictions
and set myself free.*

*I approve of myself and
the way I am changing.*

I am more powerful than my addictions.

I now discover how wonderful I am.

I choose to love and enjoy myself.

It is safe for me to be alive.

I FLOW WITH THE CHANGES TAKING PLACE IN MY LIFE

In the infinity of life where I am,
all is perfect, whole, and complete.
I see any resistance patterns within me
only as something else to release.
They have no power over me.
I am the power in my world.
I flow with the changes taking
place in my life as best I can.
I approve of myself and the way I am changing.
I am doing the best I can. Each day gets easier.
I rejoice that I am in the rhythm
and flow of my ever-changing life.
Today is a wonderful day.
I choose to make it so.
All is well in my world.

In Loving Myself, I Heal My Life

One afternoon, Louise and Robert Holden decided to take a walk in Balboa Park. As they were heading to the Japanese Friendship Garden, he asked Louise about the Hayride Reunion that had just taken place. It celebrated the 30th anniversary of Louise's support group for AIDS that became known as the Hayride. The reunion was held at the Wilshire Ebell Theatre in Los Angeles. The theater was full of friends, old and new, who came from all over the world to be there.

Suddenly they heard someone shout, "Ms. Hay! Ms. Hay!" They looked up and saw two men, arm in arm, waving at them. They were by the entrance to the Japanese Friendship Garden. As they approached, one of the men said, "Ms. Hay, I'm a Hayrider!" Louise and the man both burst into tears. They hugged each other for a long time. Robert took lots of pictures. Louise looked so happy. This man had attended Hayride meetings back in 1988 when he was preparing to die.

"You healed my life," he said.

"No. *You* healed your life," Louise told him.

When I Go Within, I Find All the Comfort and Wisdom I Need

At least once a day, I sit quietly and go within to connect with the wisdom and knowledge that is always there. This wisdom and knowledge is only a breath away. All the answers to all the questions I shall ever ask are sitting there waiting for me.

Meditating is a joy for me. I sit quietly, take a few deep breaths, relax, and go to that place of peace within. After a little while, I come back to the present moment refreshed and renewed and ready for life. Every day is a joyous new adventure for me because I choose to listen to my own inner wisdom. This wisdom is always available to me. It comes from the essence of that which exists behind the Universe of time, space, and change. When I meditate, I connect with the deep inner unchanging part of myself. Here I am energy. I am light. I am the answer already arrived. I am eternal Beingness being here now.

I CREATE LOVING EXPERIENCES IN MY LIFE EACH DAY

Many of us were mistreated as children and grew up with a negative view about life. (I was an abused child, too.) We are often afraid of feeling good about ourselves because this is a totally unfamiliar space. I know that people who have been battered and abused feel lots of anger and resentment. They usually have low self-esteem and do not feel "good enough." As a result, there are certain things you have acted out in your life with little or no understanding of their roots.

It is time to forgive yourself. The greater Intelligence of the Universe, that which I believe to be God, has already forgiven you; now it's your turn. We are all magnificent in the sight of God. You can choose to stop punishing yourself, or you can continue to feel like a victim of circumstances. Affirm right now: *I let go of the negative events of the past. I am worthy of having peace of mind and healthy relationships. I create loving experiences in my life each day.* Tell yourself, "I let go," every time you feel the pain and the guilt. And follow that with "I am healing this very moment."

Life Gives Me Everything I Need

Today you learn about how to defuse the power fear has over you and trust that Life is taking care of you.

1. What is the greatest fear you are experiencing now? Write it on a sticky note and put it on the left side of your mirror. Acknowledge this fear. Tell it: *I know you want to protect me. I appreciate that you want to help me. I thank you. Now I let you go. I release you, and I am safe.* Then take the note, rip it up, and toss it in the trash or flush it down the toilet.

2. Look in the mirror again and repeat these affirmations: *I am one with the Power that created me. I am safe. All is well in my world.*

3. We often hold our breath when we're frightened. If you are feeling threatened or fearful, consciously breathe. Take a few deep breaths. Breathing opens the space inside you that is your power. It straightens your spine, opens your chest, and gives your tender heart room to expand.

4. As you do this, repeat these affirmations: *I love you, [Name]. I really love you. I trust life. Life gives me everything I need. There is nothing to fear. I am safe. All is well.*

DEEP AT THE CENTER OF MY BEING, THERE IS AN INFINITE WELL OF LOVE

I open my heart to love.
It is safe for me to express love.
I am safe and secure in my love for myself.
I always have the perfect partner in my life.
I am open and receptive to a
wonderful, loving relationship.
Deep at the center of my being,
there is an infinite well of love.
I have come here to learn that there is only love.
I am in a harmonious relationship with Life.
I rejoice in the love I have to share.
I am creating lots of room in my life for love.

I Am the Light of the World

Look deep within the center of your heart and find a tiny pinpoint of brilliantly colored light. It is such a beautiful color. It is the very center of your love and healing energy. Watch the little pinpoint of light begin to pulsate. As it pulsates, it expands until it fills your heart. See this light moving through your body to the top of your head and the tips of your toes and fingers. You are absolutely glowing with this beautiful colored light, with your love and your healing energy. Let your whole body vibrate with this light. Say to yourself: *With every breath I take, I am getting healthier and healthier.*

Then let this light begin to radiate out from you in all directions, so that your healing energy touches everyone who needs it. Select one place on the planet as a place you would like to help heal. It may be far away or just around the corner. Concentrate your love and light and healing energy on this place, and see it come into balance and harmony. See it whole. What we give out comes back to us multiplied. Give your love. And so it is.

THE MORE LOVE I USE AND GIVE, THE MORE I HAVE TO GIVE

*In the infinity of life where I am,
all is perfect, whole, and complete.
I live in harmony and balance with everyone I know.
Deep at the center of my being,
there is an infinite well of love.
I now allow this love to flow to the surface.
It fills my heart, my body, my mind, my
consciousness, my very being, and radiates out from
me in all directions and returns to me multiplied.
The more love I use and give, the more I have to give.
The supply is endless. The use of love makes
me feel good; it is an expression of my inner joy.
I love myself; therefore, I take loving care of my body.
I lovingly feed it nourishing foods and beverages,
I lovingly groom it and dress it, and my body lovingly
responds to me with vibrant health and energy.
I love myself; therefore, I provide for
myself a comfortable home, one that fills
all my needs and is a pleasure to be in.
I fill the rooms with the vibration of love
so that all who enter, myself included, will
feel this love and be nourished by it.*

I Am Lovingly Taken Care of by the Universe

*I love myself; therefore, I work at a job I truly
enjoy doing, one that uses my creative talents
and abilities, working with and for people I love and
who love me, and earning a good income.
I love myself; therefore, I behave and think in
a loving way to all people, for I know that which I give out
returns to me multiplied. I only attract loving people in my
world, for they are a mirror of what I am.
I love myself; therefore, I forgive and totally release
the past and all past experiences, and I am free.
I love myself; therefore, I live totally in the now,
experiencing each moment as good and knowing that
my future is bright and joyous and secure, for I am
a beloved child of the Universe, and the Universe
lovingly takes care of me now and forevermore.
All is well in my world.*

LOVING MYSELF BRINGS
OUT THE BEST IN ME

If you have always been a critical person who sees life through very negative eyes, it is going to take time for you to turn yourself around to be more loving and accepting. You will learn to be patient with yourself as you practice letting go of the criticism, which is only a habit, not the reality of your being.

Can you imagine how wonderful it would be if we could live our lives without ever being criticized by anyone? We would feel totally at ease, totally comfortable. Every morning would be a wonderful new day because everyone would love you and accept you and nobody would criticize you or put you down. You can give this happiness to yourself by becoming more accepting of the things that make you unique and special.

The experience of living with yourself can be the most wonderful experience imaginable. You can wake up in the morning and feel the joy of spending another day with you. When you love who you are, you automatically bring out the best in you.

I SAY YES TO A LIFE OF INFINITE POSSIBILITIES

The totality of possibilities is how Louise describes the consciousness of the Unconditioned Self. "It's a phrase I learned from one of my early teachers, Eric Pace," says Louise. "I met Eric at the Church of Religious Science in New York, when I was in my mid-40s. I'd recently been divorced. I was feeling unlovable and like Life didn't love me. Eric taught me that if you change your thinking, you can change your life. Each time you drop a limitation—a judgment, a criticism, a fear, a doubt— you open yourself up to the totality of possibilities that exists in the infinite intelligence of your original mind."

So how do you experience your original mind? Here's a beautiful inquiry for you. The idea is to complete the following sentence five times: *One good thing that could happen if I judged myself less is . . .* Don't edit yourself or judge your answers. Allow your original mind to speak to you. Let yourself dwell in possibility. And let the basic truth of who you are inspire and guide you.

I GET BACK IN THE DRIVER'S SEAT AND TAKE CHARGE OF MY THINKING

Most people have created a habit of constantly complaining in their mind. Each time we do this, it is an affirmation, a very negative affirmation. The more we complain, the more we find to complain about. Life always gives us what we concentrate on. The more we concentrate on what is wrong in our life, the more wrongs we will find. The more wrongs we find, the more miserable we will become. It's an endless cycle. We become a constant victim of Life.

And that's when we feel like we're stuck in a rut. That's when we need to get back in the driver's seat and take charge of our thinking.

WHEN I LOVE WHAT I DO, THE MONEY WILL COME

If you were raised with the belief that you must "work hard" to earn a living, it is time to let that belief go. Do what you love, and the money will come. Love what you do, and the money will come. You have a right to enjoy earning money. Your responsibility to Life is to participate in enjoyable activities. As you find a way to do something that you enjoy, Life will show you the way to prosperity and abundance. Almost always, that activity is playful and joyful.

Our inner guidance never gives us "shoulds." The purpose of life is to play. When work becomes play, it is fun and rewarding. Remember: you decide what you want your working life to be like. Create positive affirmations to achieve it. Then declare these affirmations often. You can have the working life you want!

JULY 14

I Bless My Family with Love

Affirmations for Rising Above Family Patterns

I bless my family with love.
I allow others to be themselves.
I make my own decisions.
All my relationships are enveloped in a circle of love.
I have the power to make changes.
I release all old hurts and forgive myself.
I let go of old family limitations
and awaken to Divine harmony.
All my relationships are harmonious.
I have compassion for my parents' childhood.
I release all criticism.

I JOYFULLY KEEP MY INNER CHILD SAFE AT THE CENTER OF MY BEING

Were you welcomed as a child? Were your parents really glad you were born? Were they delighted with your sexuality, or did they want the opposite sex? Did you feel you were wanted as a child? Was there a celebration when you arrived? Whatever the responses are, welcome your child now. Create a celebration. Tell it all the wonderful things you would tell a little baby who was welcomed into its new life.

What is it you always wanted your parents to tell you when you were a child? What was it they never said that you wanted to hear? All right, tell your child that very thing. Tell it to your child every day for a month while looking in the mirror. See what happens.

I NOW CHOOSE TO RELEASE
ALL HURT AND RESENTMENT

Resentment is anger that has been buried for a long time. The main problem with resentment is that it lodges in the body, usually in the same place, and in time, it seethes and eats away at the body and often turns into tumors and cancers. Therefore, repressing anger and letting it settle in our bodies is not conducive to good health. It's time to let these feelings out.

Many of us were raised in families where we weren't allowed to be angry. Women, in particular, were taught that to be angry was something *bad*. Anger was not acceptable, except for one person, usually a parent. So we learned to swallow our anger rather than express it. Again, we can now realize that we are the ones who are holding on to it. Nobody else is involved at all.

I AM AT PEACE WITH
THE GRIEVING PROCESS

The mourning process takes at least a year. When I need to, I give myself time and space to go through this natural, normal process of life. I am gentle with myself. I allow myself to go through the grief. After a year, it begins to dissipate. I am aware that I can never lose anyone because I have never owned anyone. And in what will seem like a twinkling of an eye, I will connect with that soul again. I feel surrounded by love now, and I surround them with love wherever they are. Everybody dies. Trees, animals, birds, rivers, and even stars are born and die, and so do I. And all in the perfect time-space sequence.

Every Act of Forgiveness Is an Act of Self-Love

I am one with Life, and all of Life loves and supports me. Therefore, I claim for myself an open heart filled with love. We are all doing the best we can at any given moment, and this is also true for me. The past is over and done. I am not my parents, nor their own patterns of resentment. I am my own unique self; and I choose to open my heart and allow the love, compassion, and understanding to flush out all memories of past pain. I am free to be all that I can be. This is the truth of my being, and I accept it as so. All is well in my life.

I DWELL IN A WORLD
OF LOVE AND ACCEPTANCE

We have so much love in this world and so much love in our hearts, but sometimes we forget. Sometimes we think there isn't enough or there is just a small amount. So we hoard what we have or we are afraid to let it go. We are afraid to let it out. But those of us who are willing to learn realize that the more love we allow to flow out from us, the more there is within us . . . and the more we receive. It is endless and timeless.

Love is really the most powerful healing force there is. Without love, we could not survive at all. If tiny babies are not given love and affection, they wither and die. Most of us think we can survive without love, but we cannot. Love for ourselves is the power that heals us. So we need to be as loving as we can, every day.

PROSPERITY OF EVERY
KIND IS DRAWN TO ME

Having fear about the issue of money comes from our early childhood programming. A woman at one of my workshops said that her wealthy father had always had a fear of going broke, and he passed on the fear that his money would be taken away. She grew up being afraid that she wouldn't be taken care of. Her lack of freedom with money was tied to the fact that her father manipulated his family through guilt. She had plenty of money all her life, and her lesson was to let go of the fear that she couldn't take care of herself. Even without all the money, she could still take care of herself.

Many of us have inherited the beliefs we had when we were young, but we need to go beyond our parents' limitations and fears. We need to stop repeating their beliefs to ourselves and begin to affirm that it's okay to have money and riches. If we can trust the Power within to always take care of us no matter what, we can easily flow through the lean times, knowing that we will have more in the future.

ABUNDANCE FLOWS FREELY THROUGH ME

It is essential that we stop worrying about money and stop resenting our bills. Many people treat bills as punishments to be avoided if possible; however, a bill is an acknowledgment of our ability to pay. The creditor assumes you are affluent enough and gives you the service or the product first.

I bless with love each and every bill that comes into my home. I bless with love and stamp a small kiss on each and every check I write. If you pay with resentment, money has a hard time coming back to you. If you pay with love and joy, you open the free-flowing channel of abundance. Treat your money as a friend, not as something you wad up and crush into your pocket.

I Am My Own Perfect Partner

You are with the perfect partner at the moment—yourself! Before you came to the planet this time, you chose to be who you are this lifetime. Now you get to spend your whole life with you. Rejoice in this relationship. Make it the best, most loving relationship you can have. Be loving to yourself. Love the body you chose; it will be with you all your life. If there are things about your personality you would like to change, then change them. Do so with love and laughter, lots of laughter.

This is all part of your soul's evolution. I believe this is the most exciting time to be alive. I thank God every morning when I wake up for the privilege of being here and experiencing all that is. I trust my future to be *good*.

I Welcome Miracles into My Life

Come into my garden of life and plant new thoughts and ideas that are beautiful and nourishing. Life loves you and wants you to have the very best. Life wants you to have peace of mind, inner joy, confidence, and an abundance of self-worth and self-love. You deserve to feel at ease at all times with all people and to earn a good living. So let me help you plant these ideas in your new garden. You can nourish them and watch them grow into beautiful flowers and fruits that will in turn feed and nourish you all of your life.

I Bless My Anger with Love

A while ago, I had a pain in my shoulder for a day or two. I tried to ignore it, but it wouldn't go away. Finally, I sat down and asked myself, "What is happening here? What am I feeling?"

I realized: *It feels like burning. Burning . . . Burning . . . That means anger. What are you angry about?*

I couldn't think of what I was angry about, so I said, "Well, let's see if we can find out." I put two large pillows on the bed and began to hit them with a lot of energy.

After about 12 hits, I realized exactly what I was angry about. It was so clear. So I beat the pillows even harder and made some noise and released the emotions from my body. When I got through, I felt much better, and the next day my shoulder was fine.

I GIVE MYSELF PERMISSION
TO EXPRESS MY ANGER

Depression is anger turned inward. It is also anger that you feel you do not have a right to have. For instance, you may not feel it's okay to be angry at your parent or spouse or employer or best friend. Yet you are angry. And you feel stuck. That anger becomes depression. Far too many people today suffer from depression, even chronic depression. By the time we feel that depressed, it is very difficult to get out of it. It feels so hopeless that it becomes an effort to do anything.

I don't care how spiritual you are; you have got to wash your dishes every now and then. You can't let the sink pile up with dirty dishes and say, "Oh, I'm metaphysical." It's the same with your feelings; if you want to have a mind that flows freely, then clean up your inner mental dirty dishes. One of the best ways to do this is to give yourself permission to express some of your anger so that you don't have to stay so depressed.

New Wonderful Experiences Now Enter My Life

The past has no power over me because I am willing to learn and to change. I see the past as necessary to bring me to where I am today. I am willing to begin where I am right now to clean the rooms of my mental house. I know it does not matter where I start, so I now begin with the smallest and easiest rooms, and in that way I will see results quickly.

I close the door on old hurts and old self-righteous unforgiveness. I visualize a stream before me, and I take the old, hurtful experiences and put them in the stream and see them begin to dissolve and drift downstream until they dissipate and disappear. I have the ability to let go. I am now free to create anew.

I Change My Thinking with Love

Forgiveness is a difficult area for all of us. We build up these blocks that bind us for many years. Take my hand, and together let's work on forgiving ourselves.

1. Put on music that will make you feel peaceful. Take a journal and a pen, and let your mind drift.

2. Go back into the past and think of all the things that you're angry with yourself about. Write them down. You may discover that you have never forgiven yourself for childhood humiliations. What a long time to carry a burden!

3. Now take this list and write a positive affirmation for each item. If you wrote *I'll never forgive myself for [incident]*, then your affirmation could be. *This is a new moment. I am free to let go.* Often we demand perfection of ourselves and are harder on ourselves than on others. It's time to go beyond this old attitude. Forgive yourself. Let it go. Allow yourself to be spontaneous and free.

4. Now put down your journal and go outside—to a beach, a park, even an empty lot—and let yourself run. Don't jog; run—wild and free. Do somersaults. Skip along the street and laugh while you're doing it! Take your inner child outdoors with you and have some fun. So what if someone sees you? This is for your freedom!

LIFE IS A JOY AND FILLED WITH LOVE

These are some of the beliefs that can really help you in your life if you think or say them every day:

I am always safe.

Everything I need to know is revealed to me.

*Everything I need comes to me
in the perfect time-space sequence.*

Life is a joy and filled with love.

I prosper wherever I turn.

I am willing to change and to grow.

All is well in my world.

MY GOOD IS
CONSTANTLY COMING TO ME

We must learn to be kind to our minds. Let's not hate ourselves for having negative thoughts. We can think of our thoughts as *building* us up rather than *beating* us up. We don't have to blame ourselves for negative experiences. We can learn from these experiences. Being kind to ourselves means we stop all blame, all guilt, all punishment, and all pain.

Relaxation can help us as well. Relaxation is absolutely essential for tapping into the Power within, because if you are tense and frightened, you shut off your energy. It only takes a few minutes a day to allow the body and the mind to let go and relax. At any moment you can take a few deep breaths, close your eyes, and release whatever tension you're carrying. As you exhale, become centered and say to yourself silently: *I love you. All is well.* You will notice how much calmer you feel. You are building messages that say you don't have to go through life tense and frightened all the time.

I Am Worth Loving

You don't have to earn love any more than you have to earn the right to breathe. You have a right to breathe . . . because you exist. You have a right to be loved . . . because you exist. That is all you need to know. You are worthy of your own love. Don't allow society's negative opinions, or your parents or friends, to make you think that you are not good enough. The reality of your being is that you are lovable. Accept this and know this. When you really do, you will find that people treat you as a lovable person.

I FREE MYSELF AND EVERYONE IN MY LIFE FROM OLD PAST HURTS

Affirmations for Overcoming Abuse

*I release the past and allow
time to heal every area of my life.*

*I forgive others, I forgive myself,
and I am free to love and enjoy life.*

*I begin now to allow the child inside to
blossom and to know that it is deeply loved.*

I deserve to have boundaries and to have them respected.

I am a valued human being.

I am always treated with respect.

I release the need to blame anyone, including myself.

I deserve the best in my life, and I now accept the best.

I free myself and everyone in my life from old past hurts.

*I now choose to eliminate all negative
thoughts and see only my own magnificence.*

FORGIVING MAKES ME
FEEL FREE AND LIGHT

In the infinity of life where I am,
all is perfect, whole, and complete.
Change is the natural law of my life.
I welcome change. I am willing to change.
I choose to change my thinking.
I choose to change the words I use.
I move from the old to the new with ease and with joy.
It is easier for me to forgive than I thought.
Forgiving makes me feel free and light.
It is with joy that I learn to love myself more and more.
The more resentment I release,
the more love I have to express.
Changing my thoughts makes me feel good.
I am learning to choose to make
today a pleasure to experience.
All is well in my world.

I Think Loving Thoughts and Create a Life I Love

"I don't change anyone's life," says Louise. "Only you can change your own life."

"So what do you do?" Robert Holden asks.

"I teach people that the mind is very creative and that when you change the way you think, it will change your life."

"So you teach people how to think," he replies.

"Until someone can show you the connection between your outer experiences and your inner thoughts, you will be a victim of life," she says.

"They will feel like the world is against them," he says.

"The world isn't against us, though," says Louise. "The truth is that we are all lovable and Life loves us."

"This awareness opens us up to the totality of possibilities," he suggests.

"The totality of possibilities is always here for us," says Louise.

LOVE ALWAYS DISSOLVE PAIN

My Higher Self shows me the way to live a pain-free life. I am learning to respond to pain as if it were an alarm clock signaling me to wake up to my inner wisdom. If I have pain, I start right away with my mental work. I often replace the word pain *with the word* sensation. *My body is having a lot of "sensations." This little shift in words helps me focus my consciousness on healing, which helps me heal much quicker. I know that as I alter my mind just a little bit, my body is altered in a similar direction. I love my body, and I love my mind, and I am thankful that they are so closely related.*

LIFE SUPPORTS ME IN
EVERY POSSIBLE WAY

Heavy dependence upon anything outside myself is addiction. I can be addicted to drugs and alcohol, to sex and tobacco; and I can also be addicted to blaming people, to illness, to debt, to being a victim, to being rejected. Yet I can move beyond these things. Being addicted is giving up my power to a substance or a habit. I can always take my power back. This is the moment I take my power back!

I choose to develop the positive habit of knowing that Life is here for me. I am willing to forgive myself and move on. I have an eternal spirit that has always been with me, and it is here with me now. I relax and let go, and I remember to breathe as I release old habits and practice positive new ones.

I Cherish My Meditation Times

Some people think that if they meditate, they have to stop their minds from thinking. We really can't stop the mind, but we can slow down our thoughts and let them flow through. Some people sit with a pad and pencil and write down their negative thoughts because they seem to dissipate more easily. If we can get to a state where we are watching our thoughts float by—*Oh, there's a fear thought, and some anger, now there is a love thought, and now a disaster, there's an abandonment thought, a joy thought*—and don't give them importance, we begin to use our tremendous power wisely.

You can begin meditation anywhere and allow it to become a habit. Think of meditation as focusing on your Higher Power. You become connected with yourself and your inner wisdom. You can do it in whatever form you like. Some people go into a kind of meditation while they are jogging or walking. Again, don't make yourself wrong for doing it differently. I love to get on my knees in the garden and dig in the dirt. It's a great meditation for me.

I CHOOSE MY THOUGHTS AND CHANGE MY LIFE

We are Light. We are Spirit. We are wonderful, capable beings, all of us. And it is time for us to acknowledge that we create our own reality. We create our reality with our minds. If we want to change our reality, then it's time for us to change our minds. We do this by choosing to think and speak in new and positive ways.

I learned a long time ago that if I would change my thinking, I could change my life. Changing our thinking is really dropping our limitations. As we drop our limitations, we begin to be aware of the infinity of life all around us. We begin to understand that we are already perfect, whole, and complete. Each day gets easier.

I Am Divinely Guided and Protected at All Times

Affirmations for Spiritual Well-Being

The Power that created the world beats my heart.
I have a strong spiritual connection.
Life supports me at every turn.
I feel at one with all of Life.
I believe in a loving God.
I trust Life to be there for me.
I have a special guardian angel.
I am Divinely guided and protected at all times.
I am always progressing on the path of spiritual growth.
I am connected with Divine Wisdom.

I Am the Perfect Me

I believe that each lifetime before we are born we choose our country, our color, our sexuality, and the perfect set of parents to match the patterns we have chosen to work on in this lifetime. Each lifetime I seem to choose a different sexuality. Sometimes I am a man; sometimes I am a woman. Sometimes I am heterosexual; sometimes I am homosexual. Each form of sexuality has its own areas of fulfillment and challenges. Sometimes society approves of my sexuality, and sometimes it does not. Yet at all times I am me—perfect, whole, and complete. My soul has no sexuality. It is only my personality that has sexuality. I love and cherish every part of my body, including my genitals.

AUGUST 9

Love Is Everywhere,
and I Am Loving and Lovable

The Universal Power never judges or criticizes us. It only accepts us at our own value. Then it reflects our beliefs in our lives. If I want to believe that life is lonely and that nobody loves me, then that is what I will find in my world.

However, if I am willing to release that belief and to affirm for myself that *love is everywhere, and I am loving and lovable*, and to hold on to that new affirmation and to repeat it often, then it will become true for me. Now, loving people will come into my life, the people already in my life will become more loving to me, and I will find myself easily expressing love to others.

LOVE IS MY TEACHER

Unconditional love is the goal I think we have come here to attain. It begins with self-acceptance and self-love.

You are not here to please other people or to live your life their way. You can only live it your own way and walk your own pathway. You have come to fulfill yourself and express love on the deepest level. You are here to learn and grow and to absorb and project compassion and understanding. When you leave the planet, you don't take your relationship or your automobile or your bank account or your job with you. The only thing you take is your capacity to love!

Every Relationship Is a Mirror

Relationships are mirrors of ourselves. What we attract to ourselves will mirror either beliefs we have about relationships or qualities we have. The things we don't like about our friends are reflections of either what we do or what we believe. We could not attract such people if the way they are didn't somehow complement our own lives.

When the bond between friends becomes strained, we can look to the negative messages of childhood to understand why. For instance, if we have a friend who is undependable and lets us down, we need to turn within. We need to see where we are undependable and when we let others down. Then, we need to perform a mental housecleaning, removing the negative messages and learning to accept ourselves so that we can accept others.

Every Experience I Have Is Perfect for My Growth

No one wants to be in pain, but if you have it, what can you learn from it? Where does pain come from? What is it trying to tell you? Let's affirm: *I love my body. I return my body to optimal health by giving it what it needs on every level.*

1. When you feel pain or discomfort, take time to quiet yourself. Trust that your Higher Power will let you know what needs to be changed in your life so you can be free of this pain.

2. Visualize a perfect natural setting with your favorite flowers growing in abundance all around you. Feel and smell the sweet, warm air as it blows gently across your face. Concentrate on relaxing every muscle in your body.

3. Ask yourself these questions: *How am I contributing to this problem? What is it that I need to know? What areas of my life are in need of change?* Meditate on these questions and let the answers arise. Write down the answers in your journal.

4. Choose one of the answers you received in Step 3 and write an action plan that you can work on today.

I HELP CREATE A WORLD WHERE IT IS SAFE TO LOVE EACH OTHER

We can help create a world where it is safe for us to love each other—where we can be loved and accepted exactly as we are. It is something we all wanted when we were children—to be loved and accepted exactly as we were. Not when we got taller or brighter or prettier, or more like our cousin or sister or neighbor across the way. But to be loved and accepted exactly as we were.

We grow up and want the same—to be loved and accepted exactly as we are right here and right now. But we are not going to get it from other people unless we can give it to ourselves first. When we can love ourselves, it becomes easier for us to love other people. When we love ourselves, we don't hurt ourselves and we don't hurt other people. We let go of all prejudices and beliefs about one group or another not being good enough. When we realize how incredibly beautiful we all are, we have the answer to world peace—a world where it is safe for us to love each other.

PROSPERITY IS MY DIVINE RIGHT

Affirmations for Prosperity

Prosperity is my Divine right.
I am constantly increasing my conscious
awareness of abundance, and this reflects
in a constantly increasing income.
My good comes from everywhere and everyone.
I deserve and willingly accept an abundance
of prosperity flowing through my life.
I now establish a new awareness of success.
I know I can be as successful
as I make up my mind to be.
I rejoice in the successes of others,
knowing there is plenty for us all.
All my needs and desires are met before I even ask.
Prosperity of every kind is drawn to me.

I Awaken Today Appreciating Everything in Sight

When you get up, it's important to do a ritual that feels good to you and to say something to yourself that makes you feel good. Set in motion the best day possible for yourself. Let's affirm: *Today I create a wonderful new day and a wonderful new future.*

1. When you first wake up in the morning and open your eyes, say these affirmations to yourself: *Good morning, bed. Thank you for being so comfortable. I love you. This is a blessed day. All is well. I have time for everything I need to do today.*

2. Now take a few more minutes to relax and let these affirmations flow through your mind, then feel them in your heart and throughout the rest of your body.

3. When you're ready to get up, go to your bathroom mirror. Look deeply into your eyes. Smile at that beautiful, happy, relaxed person looking back at you!

4. As you're looking in the mirror, say these affirmations: *Good morning, [Name]. I love you. I really, really love you. There are great experiences coming our way today.* And then say something nice to yourself like: *Oh, you look wonderful today. You have the best smile. I wish you a terrific day today.*

I Love and Care for My Inner Child

We can't love and accept each other until we love and accept that lost child within us. How old is the little lost child within you? Three, four, five? Usually, the child is less than five years old because that is generally when the child shuts down out of the need to survive.

Take your child by the hand, and love it. Create a wonderful life for you and your child. Say to yourself: "I'm willing to learn to love my child. I am willing." The Universe will respond. You will find ways to heal your child and yourself. If we want to heal, we must be willing to feel our feelings and move through them to the other side for the healing. Remember, our Higher Power is always available to support us in our efforts.

I MOVE WITH EASE
THROUGH TIME AND SPACE

I have always had a streak of stubbornness within me. Even now sometimes when I decide to make a change in my life, this stubbornness can come to the surface, and my resistance to changing my thinking is strong. I can temporarily become self-righteous, angry, and withdrawn.

Yes, this still goes on within me after all these years of work. It's one of my lessons. However, when this happens now, I know I'm hitting an important point of change. Every time I decide to make a change in my life, to release something else, I'm going ever deeper into myself to do this.

Each old layer must give way in order to be replaced with new thinking. Some of it is easy, and some of it is like trying to lift a boulder with a feather. The more tenaciously I hold on to an old belief when I say I want to make a change, the more I know this is an important one for me to release. It is only by learning these things that I can teach others.

I Go Within and Connect with My Higher Intelligence

Meditation is a way of bypassing the chatter of the mind to go to the deeper levels, to connect with the inner wisdom. We are worthy of taking time each day to get in touch with the inner voice, to listen to the answers that come from the inner master. If we don't, then we are only operating on 5 to 10 percent of what is really available to us.

There are many methods of learning to meditate. There are all sorts of classes and books. It could be as simple as sitting in silence with the eyes closed for a short period of time. Remember, meditation is merely a way of you getting in touch with your own inner guidance. While we are always connected with this guidance as we go about our day, it is easier for us to consciously connect when we sit quietly and listen.

I CREATE ONLY JOYFUL EXPERIENCES IN MY LOVING WORLD

It is exciting to have wonderful people, places, and things in our lives. However, we must be clear that these things do not "make us happy." Only *we* can "make us happy." Only we can think the thoughts that can create peace and joy. Never give power to an outside person or source. Make yourself happy, and all good will flow to you in great abundance.

I Am One with the Power That Created Me

There is One Infinite Power in the Universe, and this Power is right where I am. I am not lost or alone or abandoned or helpless. I am one with the Power that created me. If there is any belief within me that would deny this truth, then I erase it right here and now. I know I am a Divine, magnificent expression of Life. I am one with Infinite Wisdom, Love, and Creativity. I am an example of vibrant health and energy. I am loving and loved. I am peaceful. This day is a glorious expression of Life. Each experience I have is joyous and loving. I bless with Divine love my body, my pets, my home, my work, and each and every person I come into contact with today. This is a great day, and I rejoice in it! And so it is!

I Am a Magnet for Miracles

Unknown and unexpected good is coming my way this day. I am far more than rules and regulations—restrictions and limitations. I change my consciousness, forgive those I need to forgive, and healing miracles occur.

Within every medical establishment there are practitioners who are enlightened and on a spiritual pathway. I now attract these people to me wherever I am. My mental atmosphere of love, acceptance, and forgiveness is a magnet for small miracles every moment of the day. Wherever I am, there is a healing atmosphere, and it blesses and brings peace to me and to all those around me.

THE LOVE OF THE UNIVERSE SURROUNDS ME AND INDWELLS ME

I am steady and secure as I connect with the One Infinite Intelligence, the Eternal Power that created me and everything else in existence throughout the Universe. I feel this Power within me. Every nerve and cell in my body recognizes this Power as good. The reality of my being is always connected with the Power that created me regardless of what any religion tells me. The savior of my life is within me. As I accept myself and know that I am good enough, I open myself to the healing power of my own love. The love of the Universe surrounds me and indwells me. I am worthy of this love. Love is now flowing through my life. Find a concept of God that supports you.

LOVING OTHERS IS EASY WHEN
I LOVE AND ACCEPT MYSELF

All of the important work we do is on ourselves. Wanting your mate to change is a subtle form of manipulation, a desire to have power over him or her. It may even be self-righteousness, because it is saying that you are better than he or she is. Allow your partners in life to be as they choose to be. Encourage their self-exploration, self-discovery, self-love, self-acceptance, and self-worth.

I Praise Myself for
Big and Little Things

Today you learn to break the habit of judgment and self-criticism, and to go beyond the need to put yourself down.

1. Make a list of five things you criticize yourself for.

2. Go down the list, and beside each item write the date on which you began to criticize yourself for this particular thing. If you can't remember the exact date, approximate.

3. Are you amazed at how long you've been picking on yourself? This habit of self-criticism has not produced any positive changes, has it? Criticism doesn't work! It only makes you feel bad. So be willing to stop it.

4. Change each of the five criticisms on your list to a positive affirmation.

I Am Learning to Be More Creative Every Day

You can never express yourself creatively by talking or thinking about what a klutz you are. If you say, "I am not creative," then that's an affirmation that will be true for you for as long as you continue to use it. There's an innate creativity flowing through you, and if you let it out, it will surprise and delight you. You're tapped into the creative flow of energy in the Universe. Some of you may express yourself more creatively than others, but everyone can do it.

We create our lives every day. Each of us has unique talents and abilities. Unfortunately, too many of us had well-meaning adults stifle that creativity when we were children. I had a teacher who once told me I couldn't dance because I was too tall. A friend was told he couldn't draw because he drew the wrong tree. It's all so silly. But we were obedient children and believed the messages. Now we can go beyond them.

MY JOB IS TO EXPRESS GOD

My job is to express God. I rejoice in this employment. I give thanks for every opportunity to demonstrate the power of Divine Intelligence to work through me. Anytime I am presented with a challenge, I know that it is an opportunity from God, my employer; and I quiet my intellect, turn within, and wait for positive words to fill my mind. I accept these blessed revelations with joy and know that I am worthy of my just reward for a job well done.

In exchange for this exhilarating position, I am abundantly compensated. My fellow employees—all of humankind—are supportive, loving, cheerful, enthusiastic, and powerful workers in the field of spiritual unfoldment, whether they choose to be aware of it or not. I see them as perfect expressions of the One Mind diligently applying themselves to their jobs. Working for this unseen yet ever-present Chief Operating Officer, the Ultimate Chairman of the Board, I know that my creative activity elicits financial abundance, for the job of expressing God is ever rewarded.

I BLESS AND PROSPER EVERYONE IN MY WORLD, AND EVERYONE IN MY WORLD BLESSES AND PROSPERS ME

Your prosperity consciousness is not dependent on money; your flow of money is dependent upon your prosperity consciousness. As you can conceive of more, more will come into your life.

I love the visualization of standing at the seashore looking out at the vast ocean and knowing that this ocean is the abundance that is available to me. Look down at your hands and see what sort of container you are holding. Is it a teaspoon, a thimble with a hole in it, a paper cup, a glass, a tumbler, a pitcher, a bucket, a washtub, or perhaps you have a pipeline connected to this ocean of abundance? Look around you and notice that no matter how many people there are and no matter what kind of container they have, there is plenty for everyone. You cannot rob another, and they cannot rob you. And in no way can you drain the ocean dry. Your container is your consciousness, and it can always be exchanged for a larger container. Do this exercise often, to get the feelings of expansion and unlimited supply.

I See the Planet Healed and Whole

Come with me as we see ourselves and our planet in new and powerful ways.

Envision a world where everyone has dignity, where everyone, no matter what race or nationality, feels empowered and secure.

See children everywhere being treasured and valued as all child abuse disappears. See schools using their precious time to teach children important things like how to love themselves, how to have relationships, how to be parents, how to handle money and be secure financially.

Then see all the sick people being made well again, dis-ease becoming a thing of the past as doctors learn to keep people healthy and vital.

All over the world, see everyone enjoying peace and plenty, with harmony among all people. As we lay down our arms and open our hearts, see judgment, criticism, and prejudice becoming old-fashioned and fading away.

See the planet, our Mother Earth, healed and whole, natural disasters dissipating as the earth breathes a sigh of relief and peace reigns.

Think about other positive things you would like to see happening on this planet. As you continue to hold these ideas in your mind and envision them, you are helping to create this new safe and loving world.

WE ARE ALWAYS SAFE;
IT IS ONLY CHANGE

Dearest One,

Here are some thoughts I have about the perfectly normal, natural process of leaving the planet—a process we will all go through. The more peaceful we can be with this experience, the easier it will be. Here's what I know:

We are always safe.
It is only change.
From the moment we are born, we are preparing
to be embraced by the Light once more.
Position yourself for maximum peace.
Angels surround you.
They are guiding you each step of the way.
However you choose your exit will be perfect for you.
Everything will happen in the perfect time-space sequence.
This is a time for joy and for rejoicing.
You are on your way home, as we all are.

I Am on an Endless Journey through Eternity

In the infinity of life, all is perfect, whole, and complete. The cycle of Life is also perfect, whole, and complete. There is a time of beginning, a time of growth, a time of being, a time of withering or wearing out, and a time of leaving. These are all part of the perfection of Life. We sense it as normal and natural, and though saddened at times, we accept the cycle and its rhythms.

Sometimes there is a sudden abrupt ending midcycle. We are jarred and feel threatened. Someone died too young, or something was smashed and broken. Often thoughts that create pain remind us of our mortality—we, too, have an ending to our cycle. Shall we live out its fullness, or will we too have an early ending?

Life is ever changing. There is no beginning and no end, only a constant cycling and recycling of substance and experience. Life is never stuck or static or stale, for each moment is ever new and fresh. Every ending is a new point of beginning.

I Trust My Body to Guide Me

The following affirmations are a great way to let your body know that you are listening. Use these for mirror work and throughout the day:

I listen with love to my body's messages.
I trust my body to guide me.
I appreciate my body's wisdom.
It is safe to listen to my body and my intuition.
Life loves me. My body loves me.
I am always guided and protected.
I know what is true for me.
I recognize my own true worth.
I nourish myself by taking in new ideas.
Life supplies everything I need.
Hi, body, we can change. I want to
hear you—let's be friends. I want to love you.

THIS IS A NEW DAY, AND I AM A NEW ME

In the infinity of life where I am,
all is perfect, whole, and complete. My life is ever new.
Each moment of my life is new and fresh and vital.
I use my affirmative thinking to create exactly what I want.
This is a new day. I am a new me.
I think differently. I speak differently. I act differently.
Others treat me differently.
My new world is a reflection of my new thinking.
It is a joy and a delight to plant new seeds, for I
know these seeds will become my new experiences.
All is well in my world.

My Best Relationship Is the One I Have with Me

Relationships are wonderful, and marriages are wonderful, but they're all temporary because there comes a time when they end. The one person I am with forever is me. My relationship with me is eternal, so I am my own best friend. I spend a little time each day connecting with my heart. I quiet down and feel my own love flowing through my body, dissolving fears and guilt. I literally feel love soaking into every cell in my body. I know that I am always connected to a Universe that loves me and everyone else unconditionally. This unconditionally loving Universe is the Power that created me, and it is always here for me. As I create a safe place in myself for love, I draw to me loving people and loving experiences. It is time to let go of my "stuff" about how relationships are supposed to be.

I FLOW WITH LIFE

You're Divinely guided by Spirit at all times. Know that Spirit makes no mistakes. When there's a strong desire within you to express or create something, know that this feeling is Divine discontent. Your longing is your calling—and no matter what it is, if you go with it, you'll be guided, guarded, and assured of success. When a purpose or path is laid before you, you have the choice to just trust and let it flow, or remain stuck in fear. Trusting the perfection that resides within you is the key. I know that it can be frightening! Everybody is afraid of something, but you can do it anyway. Remember, the Universe loves you and wants you to succeed at everything you do.

You're expressing yourself creatively every moment of every day. You're being you in your own unique way. Knowing that, you can now release any false mental beliefs that you're not creative, and go forward with each and every project that comes to mind.

I Live in an Abundant Universe

Our pursuit of money must contribute to the quality of our lives. If it does not—that is, if we hate what we do in order to get money—then money will be useless. Prosperity involves the quality of our lives as well as any amount of money that we possess.

Prosperity is not defined by money alone; it encompasses time, love, success, joy, comfort, beauty, and wisdom. For example, you can be poor with respect to time. If you feel rushed, pressured, and harried, then your time is steeped in poverty. But, if you feel you have all of the time you need to finish any task at hand, and you are confident that you can finish any job, then you are prosperous when it comes to time.

Know that whatever your beliefs are, they can be changed in this moment. The Power that created you has given you the power to create your own experiences. You can change!

I HAVE ALL THE TIME IN THE WORLD

Time is exactly what I make it to be. If I choose to feel rushed, then time speeds up and I do not have enough of it. If I choose to believe there is always enough time for me to do the things I want to do, then time slows down and I accomplish what I set out to do. If I find myself stuck in traffic, I immediately affirm that all of us drivers are doing our best to get there as soon as we can. I take a deep breath, bless the other drivers with love, and know that I will make it to my destination at the perfect time.

When we can see the perfection of each experience, then we are never rushed or delayed. We are in the right place at the right time, and all is well.

SEPTEMBER 6

I Am Worthy of Abundance

Everyone can take steps to dissolve the habits related to poor financial health. First, focus on feeling deserving and worthy of abundance so you can invite *and* receive more prosperity into your life. You can use affirmations such as:

I gratefully accept all the good I have in my life now.
Life loves me and provides for me.
I trust Life to take care of me.
I am worthy of abundance.
Life always provides for my needs.
Abundance flows into my life in surprising ways every day.
My income is constantly increasing.
I prosper wherever I turn.

ALL MY RELATIONSHIPS ARE ENVELOPED IN A CIRCLE OF LOVE

Envelop your family in a circle of love, whether they are living or not. Include your friends, your loved ones, your spouse, everyone from your work and your past, and all the people you would like to forgive and don't know how. Affirm that you have wonderful, harmonious relationships with everyone, where there is mutual respect and caring.

Know that you can live with dignity and peace and joy. Let this circle of love envelop the entire planet, and let your heart open so you have a space within you of unconditional love. You are worth loving. You are beautiful. You are powerful. And so it is.

I RELEASE THE PAST, AND I AM FREE

No matter what your early childhood was like, the best or the worst, you and only you are in charge of your life now. You can spend your time blaming your parents or your early environment, but all that accomplishes is to keep you stuck in victim patterns. It never helps you get the good you say you want.

Love is the biggest eraser I know. Love erases even the deepest and most painful memories because love goes deeper than anything else. If your mental images of the past are very strong, and you keep affirming, "It's all their fault," you stay stuck. Do you want a life of pain or one of joy? The choice and power are always within you. Look into your eyes, and love you and the little child within.

EVERY THOUGHT I THINK
IS CREATING MY FUTURE

It is my deep desire that the topic "How Your Thoughts Work" would be the very first subject taught in school. I have never understood the importance of having children memorize battle dates. It seems like such a waste of mental energy. Instead, we could teach them important subjects such as How the Mind Works, How to Handle Finances, How to Invest Money for Financial Security, How to Be a Parent, How to Create Good Relationships, and How to Create and Maintain Self-Esteem and Self-Worth.

Can you imagine what a whole generation of adults would be like if they had been taught these subjects in school along with their regular curriculum? Think how these truths would manifest. We would have happy people who feel good about themselves. We would have people who are comfortable financially and who enrich the economy by investing their money wisely. They would have good relationships with everyone and would be comfortable with the role of parenthood and then go on to create another generation of children who feel good about themselves. Yet within all this, each person would remain an individual expressing his or her own creativity.

I HAVE THE POWER TO CHANGE MY THOUGHTS, SO I FOCUS ON LOVE

Life is really very simple. What we give out, we get back. Every thought we think is creating our future.

It is only a thought, and a thought can be changed. I believe this is true for your health, too.

We create every so-called illness in our body, and we have the power to change our thoughts and begin to dissolve it.

Releasing resentment and negative thoughts will help dissolve even the most "incurable" health conditions.

When you don't know what else to do, focus on love. Loving yourself makes you feel good, and good health is really about feeling good.

When we really love ourselves, everything in our life works, including our health.

I AM AT HOME IN THE UNIVERSE

The new energy on the planet is loving. I spend time every day opening my mind and my heart to feel a kinship with all people. No matter where I was born or raised, no matter what color skin I have or what religion I was raised to believe in, everything and everyone is plugged into the One Power; through it all, our needs are met.

I have warm, loving, open communication with every member of my earthly family. There are those who look at life so differently; there are the younger ones, older ones, gay ones, straight ones, different-colored ones. I am a member of Earth's community. Differences of opinion are wonderful, colorful varieties of expression, not reason to take sides or go to war. As I dissolve prejudice in myself, the whole planet is blessed.

Today my heart opens a little more as I go about the work of creating a world where it is safe for us to love each other.

I AM HERE TO LOVE THE WORLD

"We are here to be a loving mirror to the world," Louise says. The more we love ourselves, the less we project our pain onto the world. When we stop judging ourselves, we naturally judge others less. When we stop attacking ourselves, we don't attack others. When we stop rejecting ourselves, we stop accusing others of hurting us. When we start loving ourselves more, we become happier, less defended, and more open. As we love ourselves, we naturally love others more. "Self-love is the greatest gift because what you give yourself is experienced by others," says Louise.

Love is always shared. It's a gift, like true happiness and success. It ends up benefiting you and others. "When I think about love, I like to visualize myself standing in a circle of light," says Louise. "This circle represents love, and I see myself surrounded by love. Once I feel this love in my heart and in my body, I see the circle expanding to fill the room, and then every square inch of my home, and then the neighborhood, and then the whole city, and then the whole country, and then the whole planet, and eventually, the whole Universe. That's how love is, to me. That's how love works."

THE LOVE I CREATE FOR MYSELF NOW STAYS WITH ME FOR THE REST OF MY LIFE

It is crucial to our own well-being to constantly love and appreciate the magnificent beings that we are. Our body, or the suit that we have chosen to wear in this lifetime, is a wondrous invention. It is just perfect for us. The intelligence within us beats our hearts, gives breath to our body, and knows how to heal a cut or a broken bone. Everything that goes on in our body is miraculous. If we would honor and appreciate every part of our bodies, then our health would greatly improve.

If there is some part of your body that you are not happy with, then take a month and continually put love into that area. Literally tell your body that you love it. You might even apologize for having hated it in the past. This exercise may sound simplistic, but it works. Love yourself inside and out.

The love you create for yourself now will stay with you for the rest of your life. Just as we learned to hate ourselves, so too can we learn to love ourselves. It only takes willingness and a bit of practice.

THE MORE I LOVE MY BODY, THE HEALTHIER I FEEL

Affirmations for Preparing Meals

Planning healthy meals is a joy.

*I have everything I need to help
me prepare delicious, nutritious meals.*

*I am so grateful to be choosing
food that supports my best health.*

I can easily make a nutritious, delicious meal.

I love spending time in the kitchen!

I am worth the time and money I invest in my health.

Hi, body, what would nourish you today?

*I love selecting foods that work
in harmony with you, body.*

*I am so fortunate that I can
choose healthy foods for my family.*

My family loves to eat healthy food.

The kids love to try new foods.

*I am learning new things that
heal my body one step at a time.*

*Every time I prepare food, I am nourished
by my connection to nature and other beings.*

I am willing to take this time to nurture myself.

SEPTEMBER 15

MY INNER CHILD WANTS
TO GROW AND BLOSSOM

Introduce yourself to your inner child. Find time to hold this child in your arms and let it know how safe and loved it is. I am so proud of you for taking this enormous step toward loving yourself.

1. Find a photo of yourself as a child at a time when you were truly happy. Perhaps you have a snapshot taken at your birthday party, or while you were doing something with friends or visiting one of your favorite places.

2. Tape this photo to your bathroom mirror.

3. Talk to that vibrant and happy child in the photo. Tell this child how much you want to feel that way again. Discuss with your inner child your true feelings and what's holding you back.

4. Say these affirmations to yourself: *I am willing to let go of all my fears. I am safe. I love my inner child. I love you. I am happy. I am content. And I am loved.*

5. Repeat these affirmations 10 times.

SELF-LOVE HELPS ME MAKE POSITIVE CHANGES EASILY

There is an incredible power and intelligence within you constantly responding to your thoughts and words. As you learn to control your mind by the conscious choice of thoughts, you align yourself with this power.

Do not think your mind is in control. You are in control of your mind. You use your mind. You can stop thinking those old thoughts.

When your old thinking tries to come back and say, "It's so hard to change," take mental control. Say to your mind, "I now choose to believe it is becoming easier for me to make changes." You may have to have this conversation with your mind several times for it to acknowledge that you are in control and that what you say goes.

I LOVE MYSELF TOTALLY IN THE NOW

Many of us come from dysfunctional homes. We carry over a lot of negative feelings about who we are and our relationship to life. Our childhood may have been filled with abuse, and perhaps that abuse has continued into our adult lives. When we learn early about fear and abuse, we often continue to re-create those experiences as we grow up. We may be harsh with ourselves, interpreting the lack of love and affection to mean that we are bad and deserve such abuse. We need to realize that we have the power to change all of this.

All the events we have experienced in our lifetime up to the present moment have been created by our thoughts and beliefs from the past. We do not want to look back on our lives with shame. We want to look at the past as part of the richness and fullness of life. Without this richness and fullness, we would not be here today. There is no reason to beat ourselves up because we didn't do better. We did the best we knew how. We often survived dreadful circumstances. We now can release the past in love and be grateful that it has brought us to this new awareness.

My Goal Is to Love Myself More Today Than Yesterday

The past only exists in our minds and in the way we choose to look at it in our minds. This is the moment we are living. This is the moment we are feeling. This is the moment we are experiencing. What we are doing right now is laying the groundwork for tomorrow. So this is the moment to make the decision. We can't do anything tomorrow, and we can't do it yesterday. We can only do it today. What is important is what we are choosing to think, believe, and say right now.

As we learn to love ourselves and trust our Higher Power, we become co-creators with the Infinite Spirit of a loving world. Our love for ourselves moves us from being victims to being winners. Our love for ourselves attracts wonderful experiences to us.

I Believe in the Power of Love

Love goes deeper than violence. Love lives in the heart of every human being on this earth. Wherever there is violence on this earth, love is the deeper issue trying to be heard. I am learning to listen to this silent cry within every violent report. I believe in the tools of my mind, and with these tools I move out of bondage with respect to negative experiences and into new, positive possibilities.

Many people have not been taught how to use their minds as creative instruments, so they live under whatever beliefs they were raised with. Beliefs are very powerful. People fight and kill to justify and protect their beliefs. And yet beliefs are only thoughts, and thoughts can be changed.

I love myself; therefore, I no longer violate myself or anyone else with cruel thoughts, harsh criticism, or severe judgments. I love myself; therefore, I let go of all punishing thoughts. I love myself; therefore, I give up the victim role and the victimizer role wherever I might have played these out. I forgive myself and I forgive others.

I Am Open and Receptive to All Good

Stand up with your arms outstretched and say, "I am open and receptive to all good." How does that feel?

Now, look into the mirror and say it again with more feeling.

What kinds of feelings come up for you? Does it feel liberating and joyous? Or do you feel like hiding?

Breathe deeply. Say again, "I am open and receptive to _____ [you fill in the blank]."

Do this exercise every morning. It is a wonderfully symbolic gesture that may increase your prosperity consciousness and bring more good into your life.

I CHOOSE A PEACEFUL WAY OF LIFE

If I want to live in a peaceful world, then it is up to me to make sure I am a peaceful person. No matter how others behave, I keep peace in my heart. I declare peace in the midst of chaos or madness. I surround all difficult situations with peace and love. I send thoughts of peace to all troubled parts of the world. If I want the world to change for the better, then I need to change the way I see the world. I am now willing to see life in a very positive way. I know that peace begins with my own thoughts. As I continue to have peaceful thoughts, I am connected with like-minded, peaceful-thinking people. Together we will help bring peace and plenty to our world.

My Body Is a Good Friend That I Take Loving Care Of

I forgive myself for not treating my body well in the past. I was doing the best I could with the understanding and knowledge I had. Now I care enough for myself to nourish myself with all the best that Life has to offer.

I give my body what it needs on every level to bring it up to optimal health. I eat nutritious foods with joy. I drink lots of nature's pure water. I continually find new ways to exercise that are fun. I love every part of my body, inside and out. I now choose the peaceful, harmonious, loving thoughts that create an internal atmosphere of harmony for the cells in my body to live in. I am in harmony with every part of life.

My body is a good friend that I take loving care of. I am nurtured and nourished. I rest well. I sleep peacefully. I awaken with joy. Life is good, and I enjoy living it. And so it is!

As I Change My Thoughts, the World around Me Changes

Whatever the problem is, it comes from a thought pattern, and *thought patterns can be changed*!

It may feel true, it may seem true—all these problems we're wrestling with and juggling in our lives. However, no matter how difficult an issue we are dealing with, it is only an outer result or the effect of an inner thought pattern.

If you don't know what thoughts are creating your problems, you're in the right place now, because this book is designed to help you find out. Look at the problems in your life. Ask yourself, "What kinds of thoughts am I having that create this?"

If you allow yourself to sit quietly and ask this question, your inner intelligence will show you the answer.

I Open New Doors to Life

You are standing in the corridor of life, and behind you many doors have closed. The doors represent things you no longer do or say or think, experiences you no longer have. Ahead of you is an unending corridor of doors, each one opening to a new experience.

As you move forward, see yourself opening doors on wonderful experiences you would like to have. See yourself opening doors to joy, peace, healing, prosperity, and love. Doors to understanding, compassion, and forgiveness. Doors to freedom. Doors to self-worth and self-esteem. Doors to self-love. It is all here before you. Which door will you open first?

Trust that your inner guide is leading you in the ways that are best for you and that your spiritual growth is continuously expanding. No matter which door opens or which door closes, you are always safe.

I Am Fulfilled in
All Areas of My Life

Learn to receive with thanks. Learn to accept because the Universe perceives our openness to receive as not just exchanging prosperity. Much of our problem stems from our inability to receive. We can give but it's so difficult to receive.

When someone gives you a gift, smile, and say thank you. If you say to the person, "Oh, it's the wrong size or the wrong color," I guarantee the person won't ever give you another gift. Accept graciously, and if it really isn't right for you, give it to somebody else who can use it.

We want to be grateful for what we do have, so that we can attract more good to us. Again, if we focus on lack, then we will draw it to us. If we are in debt, we need to forgive ourselves, not berate ourselves. We need to focus on the debt being paid off by doing affirmations and visualizations.

I Connect with the Treasures Within

Go within and change your thinking. Connect with the treasures within you, and use them. When we connect with the treasures within, then we will give to life from the magnificence of our being. Connect with your treasures *every day*.

Treat yourself special, as though you are a beloved friend. Make a date with yourself once a week and keep it. Go to a restaurant or a movie or a museum, or play a sport you particularly like. Dress up for this event. Eat from your best dishes. Wear your nicest clothes. Don't save the good stuff for company; be your own company. Allow yourself treats; pamper yourself.

Be grateful for life. Do random acts of kindness. Pay tolls for others. In a public restroom, tidy up and make it nice for the next person. Pick up trash on the beach or in a park. Give a flower to a stranger. Tell someone how much you appreciate him or her. Read to a lonely senior. Acts of kindness make us feel good.

I APPRECIATE THE
BEAUTIFUL WORLD I LIVE IN

The earth is a wise and loving mother. She provides everything we could ever want. All our needs are taken care of. There is water, food, air, and companionship. We have an infinite variety of animals, vegetation, birds, fish, and incredible beauty. We have treated this planet very badly in the last few years. We have been using up our valuable resources. If we continue to wastefully trash the planet, we will have no place to live.

I have committed to lovingly take care of and improve the quality of life in this world. My thoughts are clear and loving and concerned. I express random acts of kindness whenever I can. I recycle and compost and organically garden and improve the quality of the soil. It is my planet, and I help to make it a better place to live. I spend quiet time every day actively imagining a peaceful planet. I imagine the possibilities of a clean, healthy environment.

I envision the governments of the world working together to balance their budgets and handle money fairly. I see all the people on the planet opening their hearts and their minds and working together to create a world where it is safe for us to love each other. It is possible. And it starts with me.

I Claim My Power

Welcome this new day with open arms and love. Feel your power. Feel the power of your breath. Feel the power of your voice. Feel the power of your love. Feel the power of your forgiveness. Feel the power of your willingness to change.

You are beautiful. You are a Divine, magnificent being. You deserve all good—not just some good, but *all* good. Feel your power and be at peace with it, for you are safe.

I Am Deeply Grateful to Life
for All Its Generosity to Me

I am one with Life, and all of Life loves and supports me. Therefore, I claim for myself an abundant share of the prosperity of life. I have an abundance of time, love, joy, comfort, beauty, wisdom, success, and money. I am not my parents, nor their own financial patterns. I am my own unique self, and I choose to be open and receptive to prosperity in all its many forms. I am deeply grateful to Life for all its generosity to me. My income constantly increases, and I continue to prosper for the rest of my life. This is the truth of my being, and I accept it as so. All is well in my prosperous world.

TODAY I ENJOY EVERY MINUTE OF WHATEVER I AM DOING

In each lifetime
We always come into the middle of the movie
And we always leave in the middle of the movie.
There is no right time, there is no wrong time.
It is only our time.
The soul makes the choice long before we come in.
We have come to experience certain lessons.
We have come to love ourselves.
No matter what "they" did or said
We have come to cherish ourselves and others.
When we learn the lesson of love, we may leave with joy.
There is no need for pain or suffering.
We know that next time, wherever we choose to incarnate,
On whatever plane of action
We will take all of the love with us.

I Love Who I Am and All That I Do

In the infinity of life where I am,
all is perfect, whole, and complete.
I support myself, and life supports me.
I see evidence of the spiritual laws working all
around me and in every area of my life.
I reinforce that which I learn in joyous ways.
My day begins with gratitude and joy.
I look forward with enthusiasm
to the adventures of the day,
knowing that in my life, "All is good."
I love who I am and all that I do.
I am the living, loving, joyous expression of Life.
All is well in my world.

The Point of Power Is in the Present Moment

We can always change our belief systems. We once believed the world was flat. Now that is no longer a truth for us. I know we can change what we think and accept as normal. We can live long lives that are healthy, loving, wealthy, wise, and joyous.

My Love Is Powerful

I treat myself as if I am someone who is deeply loved. All kinds of events come and go, yet through it all, the love for myself is constant. This is not being vain or conceited. People who are vain or conceited have a lot of self-hatred covered over by a layer of "I'm better than you." Self-love is simply appreciating the miracle of my own being. When I really love myself, I cannot hurt myself, and I cannot hurt another person. To me, the answer to world peace is unconditional love. It begins with self-acceptance and self-love. I no longer wait to be perfect in order to love myself. I accept myself exactly as I am right here and now.

I Am Worthy of Being Healed

"If you put yourself in a position where you know you can be healed, the right help will come to you. Then you have to be willing to do the work," Louise says.

What does it take to put yourself in a position to attract what you need to heal?

"You first need to change your thinking about the problem. We all have ideas about healing and how things should and shouldn't work. We need to shift our thinking from *It can't be done* to *It can be done—I just have to figure out how.* I've always said that the word *incurable* means that it can't be cured by any *outer* means at the moment, so we need to go within. That, of course, would mean changing your thinking. You also need to develop self-worth—you need to believe that you are worthy of being healed. If you can develop that as a strong belief and affirmation, then Life will bring you what you need to manifest the healing."

OCTOBER 5

I Am Never Too Old
to Learn and Grow

Never make the mistake of thinking that you're too old for anything. My own life didn't begin to have meaning until I was in my mid-40s, when I started teaching. At age 50, I started my publishing company on a very small scale. At 55, I ventured into the world of computers, taking classes and overcoming my fear of them. At 60, I started my first garden and have become an avid organic gardener who grows her own food. At 70, I enrolled in a children's art class. A few years later, I graduated to an adult art class and have started to sell my paintings.

Recently, I decided to stretch myself in areas that scared me, and I took up ballroom dancing. Now I'm taking several classes a week, and I'm fulfilling my childhood dream of learning to dance. I also took up yoga, and my body is making positive changes.

I love to learn things I haven't experienced. Who knows what I'll do in the future? What I do know is that I'll be doing my affirmations and expressing new creativity until the day I leave this planet.

I CHOOSE POSITIVE THOUGHTS
THAT MAKE ME FEEL GOOD

Some people say that "affirmations don't work" (which is an affirmation in itself), when what they mean is that they don't know how to use them correctly. They may say, "My prosperity is growing," but then think, *Oh, this is stupid; I know it won't work*. Which affirmation do you think will win out? The negative one, of course, because it's part of a long-standing, habitual way of looking at life. Sometimes people will say their affirmations once a day and complain the rest of the time. It will take a long time for affirmations to work if they're done that way. The complaining affirmations will always win, because there are more of them, and they're usually said with great feeling.

However, saying affirmations is only part of the process. What you do the rest of the day and night is even more important. The secret to having your affirmations work quickly and consistently is to prepare an atmosphere in which they can grow. Affirmations are like seeds planted in soil. Poor soil, poor growth. Rich soil, abundant growth. The more you choose thoughts that make you feel good, the quicker the affirmations work.

MY INNER DIALOGUE
IS KIND AND LOVING

I have a unique role to play on this earth, and I also have the tools to do the job. The thoughts I think and the words I speak are my incredibly powerful tools. I use them and I enjoy what they produce for me! Meditation, prayer, or 10 minutes of affirmations in the morning are wonderful, and I get better results when I am consistent all day long. I remember that it's the moment-to-moment thinking that is really shaping my life. The point of power, the place where I make changes, is always right here and now. So, just for a moment, I catch the thought I'm thinking right now. And I ask myself, do I want that thought to create my future?

I Rejoice in the Love That I Have to Share

I teach one thing, and one thing only—love yourself. Until you love yourself, you will never know who you really are and you won't know what you're really capable of. When you love yourself, you grow up. Love helps you to grow beyond your past, beyond pain, beyond fears, beyond your ego, and beyond all your small ideas about yourself. Love is what you're made of, and love helps you to be who you really are.

In Every Relationship, There Is a Lesson to Learn and a Gift to Receive

I believe that you chose your parents before you were born in order to learn valuable lessons. Your Higher Self knew the experiences that were necessary for you to proceed on your spiritual course. So whatever you came to work out with your parents, get on with it. No matter what they say or do, or said or did, you are here ultimately to love yourself.

As parents, allow your children to love themselves by giving them the space to feel safe to express themselves in positive, harmless ways. Remember, too, just as we chose our parents, our children also chose us. There are important lessons for all of us to work out.

Parents who love themselves will find it easier to teach their children about self-love. When we feel good about ourselves, we can teach our children self-worth by example. The more we work on loving ourselves, the more our children will realize that it's an okay thing to do.

My Mental Pattern Is
Positive and Joyful

Some of the things we believe are positive and nourishing. These thoughts serve us well all of our lives, such as: *Look both ways before you cross the street.*

Other thoughts are very useful at the beginning, but as we grow older they are no longer appropriate. *Don't trust strangers* may be good advice for a small child, but for an adult, to continue this belief will only create isolation and loneliness.

Why do we so seldom sit down and ask ourselves, *Is that really true?* For instance, why do I believe things like *It's difficult for me to learn?*

Better questions to ask are: *Is it true for me now? Where did that belief come from? Do I still believe it because a first-grade teacher told me that over and over? Would I be better off if I dropped that belief?*

Forgiveness Sets Me Free

One of the biggest spiritual lessons to understand is that everyone is doing the best they can at any given moment. People can do only so much with the understanding and awareness they have. The incident you are holding on to is over. Let it go. Allow yourself to be free.

1. Sit in front of your mirror and close your eyes. Breathe deeply several times. Feel yourself grounded on your chair.

2. Think of the many people who have hurt you in your life. Now open your eyes and begin to talk to one of them—aloud. Say something like "You hurt me deeply. However, I will not stay stuck in the past any longer. I am willing to forgive you." If you can't do that yet, just affirm, *I am willing.* Your willingness is all it takes to move toward forgiveness.

3. Take a breath and then say to the person, "I forgive you. I set you free." Breathe again and say, "You are free. I am free."

4. Notice how you feel. Do you feel resistance, or do you feel relief? If you feel resistance, just breathe and affirm: *I am willing to release all resistance.*

5. Remember: forgiveness is not an event; it's a process. You may need to keep working on one person a little longer, each time going a little deeper into forgiveness.

I Am at Peace with My Age

*In the infinity of life where I am, all is perfect,
whole, and complete. I no longer choose
to believe in the old limitations and lack that
once defined the aging process. I rejoice in
each passing year. My wealth of knowledge
grows, and I am in touch with my wisdom.
My later years are my treasure years, and
I know how to keep myself youthful and
healthy. My body is renewed at every
moment. I am vital, vivacious, healthy, fully
alive, and contributing to my last day.
I now choose to live my life from this
understanding. I am at peace with my age.*

My Life Is Joyous No Matter What Age I Am

Affirmations for the Aging Process

I am young and beautiful—at every age.
I am open to experiencing all that life has to offer.
I contribute to society in fulfilling and productive ways.
I am in charge of my finances, my health, and my future.
I honor and respect the children and adolescents in my life.
My family is supportive of me, and I am supportive of them.
I am respected by all with whom I come in contact.
I honor and respect all the elders in my life.
I have all the time in the world.
I have no limitations.

I Am One with Everyone on the Planet

There are not two conflicting powers—that is, good and evil. There is One Infinite Spirit, and there are human beings who have the opportunity to use the intelligence and wisdom and tools they have been given in every way. When you talk about *them*, you are talking about *us*, because we are the people, we are the government, we are the churches, and we are the planet.

The place to begin making changes is right where we are. It is all too easy to say: "It's the devil" or "It's them." It really is always *us*!

I Look Within and Love What I See

How do you love yourself? First of all, and most important: cease all criticism of yourself and others. Accept yourself as you are. Praise yourself as much as you can. Criticism breaks down the inner spirit; praise builds it up. Look into a mirror often, and simply say: *I love you, I really love you.* It may be difficult at first, but keep practicing, and soon you will mean and feel what you say. Love yourself as much as you can, and all of Life will mirror this love back to you.

I Dwell on Positive Thoughts

The Universe takes your thoughts and words very literally and gives you what you say you want. Always.

Every positive thought brings good into your life. Every negative thought pushes good away; it keeps it just out of your reach. How many times in your life have you almost gotten something good and it seemed to be snatched away at the last moment? If you could remember what your mental atmosphere was like at those times, you'd have the answer. Too many negative thoughts create a barrier against positive affirmations.

If you say, "I don't want to be sick anymore," this is not an affirmation for good health. You have to state clearly what you do want. "I accept perfect health now."

"I hate this car" does not bring you a wonderful new car because you're not being clear. Even if you do get a new car, in a short time you'll probably hate it, because that's what you've been affirming. If you want a new car, then say something like this: "I have a beautiful new car that suits all of my needs."

TODAY I CHOOSE TO GIVE LOVE

Honesty is a word we use a lot, not always understanding the true significance of what it means to be honest. It has nothing to do with morality or being a goody-goody. Being honest really has little to do with getting caught or going to jail. It is an act of love for ourselves.

The main value of honesty is that whatever we give out in life we will get back. The law of cause and effect is always operating on all levels. If we belittle or judge others, then we, too, are judged. If we are always angry, then we encounter anger wherever we go. The love we have for ourselves keeps us in tune with the love Life has for us.

THE MORE I OPEN TO LOVE, THE SAFER I AM

Work on loving yourself continually every day. Say your loving affirmations every moment you can. Demonstrate the growing love you have for yourself. Pamper yourself. Show yourself how special you are. Life always mirrors back to us the feelings we have inside.

As you develop your inner sense of love and romance, the right person to share your growing sense of intimacy will be attracted to you like a magnet.

1. In your journal, write about how you experienced love as a child. Did you observe your parents expressing love and affection? Were you raised with lots of hugs? In your family, was love hidden behind fighting, crying, or silence?

2. Write 10 affirmations of love and practice them in front of your mirror. Here are some examples: *I am worthy of love. The more I open to love, the safer I am. Today I remember that life loves me. I let love find me at the perfect time.*

3. Write down 10 things that you love to do. Pick five and do them today.

4. Take several hours and pamper yourself: buy yourself flowers, treat yourself to a healthy meal, show yourself how special you are.

5. Repeat Step 3 every day this week!

My Day Begins and Ends with Gratitude and Joy

Let's spend as many moments as we can every day being grateful for all the good that is in our lives. If you have little in your life now, it will increase. If you have an abundant life now, it will increase. This is a win-win situation. You are happy, and the Universe is happy. Gratitude increases your abundance.

Start a gratitude journal. Write something to be grateful about each day. On a daily basis, tell someone how grateful you are for something. Tell sales clerks, waiters, postal workers, employers and employees, friends, family, and perfect strangers. Share the gratitude secret. Let's help make this a world of grateful, thankful giving and receiving . . . for everyone!

OCTOBER 20

I Trust the Guidance of the Universe

In the infinity of life where we all are, all is perfect, whole, and complete. We rejoice in knowing we are one with the Power that created us. This Power loves all its creations, including us. We are the beloved children of the Universe and have been given everything. We are the highest form of life on this planet and have been equipped with all that we need for every experience we shall have. Our minds are always connected to the One Infinite Mind; therefore, all knowledge and wisdom is available to us if we believe it is so.

We trust ourselves to create only that which is for our highest good and greatest joy—that which is perfect for our spiritual growth and evolution. We love who we are. We are particularly delighted with the incarnation we have chosen this lifetime. We know that we can, from moment to moment, shape and reshape our personalities and even our bodies to further express our greatest potential. We rejoice in our unlimitedness and know that before us lies the totality of possibilities in every area. We trust totally in the One Power, and we know that all is well in our world.

I TRUST LIFE TO HELP ME MAKE
WISE AND LOVING DECISIONS

Robert Holden's children, Bo and Christopher, love Louise Hay, and she feels the same way about them. It's interesting watching them together. Louise doesn't dote. She doesn't do tickles. She doesn't play games. She treats Bo, who is six years old, not as a "big girl" or a "good girl" but as a real girl. Christopher, who is three years old, is a real boy. And Louise is no age at all. And that's that. It's all perfectly natural. The way they are together reminds Robert of Mary Poppins with Jane and Michael.

The first time Christopher met Louise, he ran right up to her and shouted, "Would you like to see my teeth?" Louise considered his proposal for a moment and said, "Yes, I would." Christopher then looked up and grinned. "Thank you," said Louise. "That's okay," said Christopher. He hadn't done that with anyone before and hasn't repeated it since.

Later on, Robert asked Louise about the significance of teeth. In her matter-of-fact way, she said, "Teeth are about making good decisions. He was simply telling me that he knows his own mind and that he is capable of making good decisions."

THE FIRST RELATIONSHIP TO IMPROVE IS THE ONE WITH MYSELF

The first relationship to improve is the one you have with yourself. When you're happy with yourself, then all of your other relationships improve, too. A happy person is very attractive to others. If you're looking for more love, then you need to love yourself more. This means no criticism, no complaining, no blaming, no whining, and no choosing to feel lonely. It means being very content with yourself in the present moment and choosing to think thoughts that make you feel good now.

When you're able to contribute to the fulfillment of your own needs, then you won't be so needy and codependent. It has to do with how much you love yourself. When you truly love who you are, you stay centered, calm, and secure, and your relationships at home as well as at work are wonderful. You'll find yourself reacting to various situations and people differently. Matters that once may have been desperately important won't seem quite as crucial anymore. New people will enter your life, and perhaps some old ones will disappear—this can be kind of scary at first, but it can also be wonderful, refreshing, and exciting.

I Am Open and Receptive to All Good

When something good comes into your life, say yes to it. Open yourself to receiving good. Say yes to your world. Opportunities and prosperity will increase a hundredfold.

Today your mirror work is going to focus on receiving your prosperity.

1. Stand up with your arms outstretched and say: *I am open and receptive to all good.*

2. Now look into the mirror and say it again: *I am open and receptive to all good.* Let the words flow from your heart: *I am open and receptive to all good.*

3. Repeat this affirmation 10 more times.

4. Notice how you feel. Do you feel liberated? Do this exercise every morning for a week or more. It's a wonderful way to increase your prosperity consciousness.

TODAY I FOLLOW MY BLISS

I think that we come to this planet many, many times, and we come to learn different lessons. It's like coming to school. Before we incarnate at any particular time on the planet, we decide the lesson we are going to learn so that we can evolve spiritually. Once we choose our lesson, we choose all the circumstances and situations that will enable us to learn the lesson, including our parents, sexuality, place of birth, and race. If you've gotten this far in your life, believe me, you've made all the right choices.

As you go through life, it is essential to remind yourself that you are safe. It is only change. Trust your Higher Self to lead you and guide you in ways that are best for your spiritual growth. As Joseph Campbell once said, "Follow your bliss."

I Go from Success to Success

I know that the thoughts in my mind have everything to do with my working conditions, so I consciously choose my thoughts. My thoughts are supportive and positive. I choose prosperity thinking; therefore, I am prosperous. I choose harmonious thoughts; therefore, I work in a harmonious atmosphere. I love getting up in the morning knowing that I have important work to do today. I have challenging work that is deeply fulfilling. My heart glows with pride when I think of the work that I do. I am always employed, always productive. Life is good. And so it is!

I Am a Shining Light

Competition and comparison are two major stumbling blocks to your creativity. Your uniqueness sets you apart from all others. There has never been another person like you since time began, so what is there to compare or compete with? Comparison makes you feel either superior or inferior, which are expressions of your ego, your limited mind thinking. If you are going to compare to make yourself feel a little bit better, then you are saying somebody else isn't good enough. If you put others down, you may think you will raise yourself up. What you really do is put yourself in a position to be criticized by others. We all do this on some level, and it's good when we can transcend it. Becoming enlightened is to go within and shine the light on yourself so you can dissolve whatever darkness is in there.

Everything changes, and what was perfect for you once may not be anymore. In order for you to keep changing and growing, you keep going within and listening for that which is right for you in the here and now.

I BLESS MY TELEPHONE

I bless my telephone with love each time I use it, and I affirm often that it brings me only prosperity and expressions of love. I do the same with my mailbox, and each day it is filled to overflowing with money and love letters of all kinds from friends and clients and far-off readers of my book. The bills that come in I rejoice over, thanking the companies for trusting me to pay. I bless my doorbell and the front door, knowing that only good comes into my home. I expect my life to be good and joyous, and it is.

The Law of Attraction Brings Only Good into My Life

I have noticed that the Universe loves gratitude. The more grateful you are, the more goodies you get. When I say "goodies," I don't mean only material things. I mean all the people, places, and experiences that make life so wonderfully worth living. You know how great you feel when your life is filled with love and joy and health and creativity, and you get the green lights and the parking places. This is how our lives are meant to be lived. The Universe is a generous, abundant giver, and it likes to be appreciated.

I Am My Own Unique Self

You are not your father. You are not your mother. You are not any of your relatives. You are not your teachers at school, nor are you the limitations of your early religious training. You are yourself. You are special and unique, having your own set of talents and abilities. No one can do things exactly the way you can do them. There is no competition and no comparison. You are worthy of your own love and your own self-acceptance. You are a magnificent being. You are free. Acknowledge this as the new truth for yourself. And so it is.

WE ARE WONDERFUL SPIRITUAL BEINGS HAVING A HUMAN EXPERIENCE

I am one with Life, and all of Life loves and supports me. Therefore, I claim for myself peace of mind and joy of living for every age of my life. Each day is new and different and brings its own pleasures. I am an active participant in this world. I am an eager student with an intense desire to learn. I take excellent care of my body. I choose thoughts that make me happy. I have a strong spiritual connection that sustains me at all times. I am not my parents, nor do I have to age or die the way they did. I am my own unique self, and I choose to live a deeply fulfilling life until my last day on this planet. I am at peace with living, and I love all of Life. This is the truth of my being, and I accept it as so. All is well in my life.

I Am Willing to See Only My Own Magnificence

Choose to eliminate from your mind and your life every negative, destructive, fearful idea and thought. No longer listen to or become part of detrimental thoughts or conversations. Today no one can harm you because you refuse to believe in being hurt. You refuse to indulge in damaging emotions, no matter how justified they may seem to be. You rise above anything that attempts to make you angry or afraid. Destructive thoughts have no power over you.

You think and say only what you want to create in your life. You are more than adequate for all you need to do. You are one with the Power that created you. You are safe. All is well in your world.

WHATEVER I AM GUIDED TO DO WILL BE A SUCCESS

In the infinity of life where I am,
all is perfect, whole, and complete.
I am one with the Power that created me.
I have within me all the ingredients for success.
I now allow the success formula to flow through me
and manifest in my world.
Whatever I am guided to do will be a success.
I learn from every experience.
I go from success to success and from glory to glory.
My pathway is a series of stepping-stones
to ever-greater successes.
All is well in my world.

I TRUST THE PROCESS OF
LIFE TO TAKE CARE OF ME

Louise trusts her inner ding with her life. "It's my friend," she tells Robert Holden. "It's an inner voice that talks to me. I've learned to trust it. It's right for me." She talks about her inner ding with reverence and love. Listening to it is a daily spiritual practice. "My inner ding is always with me," she says. "When I listen to my inner ding, I find the answers I need."

"Where does your inner ding come from?" he asks.

"Everywhere!" says Louise, being playful.

"What does that mean?"

"My inner ding is how I listen to the big wisdom," she says.

"Is this like the One Intelligence you refer to in *You Can Heal Your Life*?"

"Yes, the One Intelligence that offers guidance to us all," she says.

"Do we all have an inner ding?" he asks.

"Every child is born with an inner ding," Louise assures him.

I Give My Inner Child All the Love It Has Wanted and More

Love is the greatest healing power I know. Love can heal even the deepest and most painful memories because love brings the light of understanding to the dark corners of our mind. No matter how painful our early childhood was, loving our inner child now will help us to heal it. In the privacy of our own minds we can make new choices and think new thoughts. Thoughts of forgiveness and love for our inner child will open pathways, and the Universe will support us in our efforts.

I Know That Only Good Awaits Me at Every Turn

I believe that everything does work out for the best in the end, but sometimes it is hard to see that while you are going through the experience. Think of a negative experience that may have happened to you in your work or in you past, in general. Perhaps you were fired or maybe your spouse left you. Now go beyond it and take a look at the big picture. Didn't many good things happen as a result of that experience? I've heard so many times, "Yes, that was a horrible thing that happened to me, but if it hadn't, I never would have met so-and-so . . . or started my own business . . . or admitted that I had an addiction . . . or learned to love myself."

By trusting the Divine Intelligence to let us experience life in the way that is best for us, we empower ourselves to actually enjoy *everything* that life has to offer: the good as well as the so-called bad. Try applying this to your work experiences, and notice the changes that happen to you.

My Work Is an
Expression of Divine Love

Our business is a Divine idea in the One Mind, created out of Divine love and sustained by love. Every employee has been attracted by the action of love, for it is his or her Divine right place here at this point in time and space. Divine harmony permeates us all, and we flow together in a most productive and joyous way. It is the action of love that brought us to this particular place. Divine right action operates every aspect of our business. Divine Intelligence creates our products and services. Divine love brings to us those who can be helped by that which we so lovingly do.

We release all old patterns of complaining or condemning, for we know that it is our consciousness that creates our circumstances in the business world. We know and declare that it is possible to successfully operate our business according to Divine principles, and we lovingly use our mental tools to live and experience our lives more abundantly. We refuse to be limited in any way by human-mind thinking. The Divine Mind is our business consultant and has plans for us that we have not yet dreamed. Our lives are filled with love and joy because our business is a Divine idea. And so it is.

I Am Love

We are all on an endless journey through eternity, and the time we spend on this Earth plane is but a brief instant. We choose to come to this planet to learn lessons and to work on our spiritual growth and to expand our capacity to love. There is no right time and no wrong time to come and go. We always come in the middle of the movie, and we leave in the middle of the movie. We leave when our particular task is finished. We come to learn to love ourselves more and to share that love with all those around us. We come to open our hearts on a much deeper level. Our capacity to love is the only thing we take with us when we leave. If you left today, how much would you take?

I Have the Power to
Create My Own Experiences

You have the power to alter your life so that you will not even recognize your old self. You can go from illness to health, from loneliness to love. You can go from poverty to security and fulfillment. You can go from guilt and shame to self-confidence and self-love. You can go from a feeling of worthlessness to feeling creative and powerful.

I Am in the Process of Becoming My Own Best Friend—the Person I Am Happiest to Be With

Life is sacred. I hold to my heart all the parts of myself—the infant; the child; the teenager, young adult, adult, and future self. Every embarrassment, mistake, hurt, and wound, I accept fully as part of my story. My story includes every success and every failure, every error and every truthful insight, and all of it is valuable in ways I don't have to figure out. Sometimes the painful parts of my story help other people understand their own pain. When other people share their pain with me, I feel compassion for them. I now extend this same compassion to myself. I relax in knowing everything about me is acceptable.

I JOYOUSLY GIVE TO LIFE, AND LIFE LOVINGLY GIVES BACK TO ME

Did you know that prosperity and gratitude go hand in hand? The Universe is a generous giver and likes to be appreciated. Let's affirm: *I joyously give to Life, and Life lovingly gives back to me.*

1. When you first wake up in the morning and open your eyes, say these affirmations to yourself: *Good morning, bed. I am so grateful for the warmth and comfort you have given me. Darling [Name], this is a blessed day. All is well.*

2. Take a few more minutes to relax in your bed and think of all the things you are grateful for.

3. When you're ready to get up, go to the bathroom mirror. Look sweetly and deeply into your eyes. List the many things you are grateful for. Say them as affirmations: *I am grateful for my beautiful smile. I am grateful to feel perfectly healthy today. I am grateful for having a job to go to today. I am grateful for the friends I am going to meet today.*

4. Whenever you pass a mirror today, stop and say an affirmation for something you are grateful for in that moment.

NOVEMBER 10

WHEREVER I GO I AM GREETED WITH WARMTH AND FRIENDLINESS

I am one with Life, and all of Life loves and supports me. Therefore, I claim for myself a joyous, loving circle of friends. We all have such good times individually and together. I am not my parents nor their relationships. I am my own unique self; and I choose to only allow supportive, nurturing people in my world. Wherever I go I am greeted with warmth and friendliness. I deserve the best friends, and I allow my life to be filled with love and joy. This is the truth of my being, and I accept it as so. All is well in my friendly world.

I REJOICE IN OTHERS' GOOD FORTUNE

Don't delay your own prosperity by being resentful or jealous that someone else has more than you. Don't criticize the way they choose to spend their money. It is none of your business.

Each person is under the law of his or her own consciousness. Just take care of your own thoughts. Bless another's good fortune, and know there is plenty for all.

I Am Centered in Truth and Peace

Come from that wonderful, caring spot of your heart. Stay centered and love who you are. Know that you really are a Divine, magnificent expression of Life. No matter what is going on out there, you are centered. You have a right to your feelings. You have a right to your opinions. You just are. Work on loving yourself. Work on opening your heart. Sometimes it is scary to do that because the answers you get inside may be quite different from what your friends want you to do. Yet you know inwardly what is right for you. And if you follow this inner wisdom, you are at peace with your own being.

Support yourself in making the right choices for yourself. When you are in doubt, ask yourself: "Am I coming from the loving space of my heart? Is this a decision that is nurturing for me? Is this right for me now?" The decision you make at some later point—a day, a week, or a month later—may no longer be the right choice, and then you can change it. Ask in every moment: "Is this right for me?" And say: "I love myself and I am making the right choices."

No Matter the Challenge, I Know I Am Loved

If something unpleasant happens to you during the day, immediately go to the mirror and say: "I love you anyway." Events come and go, but the love you have for yourself can be constant, and it's the most important quality you possess in life. If something wonderful happens, go to the mirror and say, "Thank you." Acknowledge yourself for creating this wonderful experience.

I ALLOW MYSELF THE TIME I NEED TO WORK THROUGH MY GRIEF

Affirmations for Death and Grief

Death is a door opening to a new life.
I am at peace with the grieving process.
I am at peace with my loved one's passing.
I allow myself the time I need to work through my grief.
Our spirit can never be taken from us,
for it is the part of us that is eternal.
Death is a natural part of life.
Everyone dies within the perfect time-space sequence.
I know that no matter where I am, I am safe
and loved and totally supported by Life.
Our spirit, our soul, is always safe,
always secure, and always alive.
I let the light of my love shine so
that it comforts me and others.
There is no death, only a change of form.

I SPEAK AND THINK POSITIVELY

When you hear yourself say, "I'm not ready," is it your soul speaking or your ego? Lots of us encounter this thought before we start something new like getting married, having a baby, creating a business, writing a book, or giving a public talk. Is it really true you're not ready? If so, get some extra help. If not, tell your ego to relax and let your soul lead the way.

We spend our life thinking *I'm not ready*, and then one day it changes. We stop thinking *I'm not ready* and start thinking *I'm too old*. Who says? How old is your soul anyway? Are you too old really, or do you feel unworthy or afraid or something else? When you watch your thoughts, and you suspend your judgments, you get to see what the real thought is.

"A thought is just an idea," Louise says. "And you are either thinking with the mind of your soul or the mind of your ego."

LOVING MYSELF OPENS THE DOOR TO POSITIVE CHANGE

My spiritual growth often comes to me in strange ways. It can be a chance meeting or an accident, a dis-ease or the loss of a loved one. Something inside urges me to follow, or I am forcefully prevented from living in the same old way. It is a little different for each person. I grow spiritually when I accept responsibility for my life. This gives me the Inner Power to make the changes in myself that I need to make. Spiritual growth is not about changing others. Spiritual growth happens to the person who is ready to step out of the victim role, into forgiveness, and into a new life. None of this happens overnight. It is an unfolding process. Loving myself opens the door, and being willing to change really helps.

ALL THAT I SEEK IS
ALREADY WITHIN ME

Your security is not your job, or your bank account, or your investments, or your spouse or parents. Your security is your ability to connect with the cosmic Power that creates all things.

I like to think that the Power within me that breathes in my body is the same Power that provides all that I need, and just as easily and simply. The Universe is lavish and abundant, and it is our birthright to be supplied with everything we need, unless we choose to believe it to the contrary.

I Live in a Friendly Universe

"What do you think about the friendly Universe idea?" Robert Holden asks Louise.

She pauses for a moment as she lets the question sink in. "I think it's a good idea," she says with a smile.

"Is the Universe friendly?" he asks Louise.

"There's only one way to find out," she says.

"What way is that?"

"Say yes," she says with a smile.

"What do you mean?"

"If you answer no, you'll never find out if the Universe is friendly," she says.

"Because if you say no, you won't see it."

"Exactly. But if you say yes, then you might."

"It's all in the answer."

"The answer is in us," says Louise.

I Am Open to New and Wonderful Changes

There is so much abundance in this world just waiting for you to experience it. If you would know that there is more money than you could ever spend, or more people than you could ever meet, and more joy than you could imagine, you would have everything you need and desire. If you ask for your highest good, then trust the Power within to provide it to you. Be honest with yourself and others. Don't cheat, not even a little; it will only come back to you.

The Infinite Intelligence that permeates all says "Yes!" to you. When something comes into your life, don't push it away, say "Yes!" to it. Open yourself to receiving good. Say "Yes!" to your world. Opportunity and prosperity will increase a hundredfold.

EVERYTHING HAPPENS IN THE PERFECT TIME-SPACE SEQUENCE

I believe we each come to this planet to learn certain lessons. When those lessons have been learned, we leave. A lesson for a certain lifetime may be a short one. Whatever way we leave and whenever we leave, I believe it is a soul choice and that it occurs in the perfect time-space sequence. Our soul allows us to leave in the way that is best for us this time around. When we see the larger picture of life, it is impossible for us to judge any one method of leaving.

I Love Taking Time to Eat Mindfully and Fully Enjoy My Meals

Affirmations for Eating Meals

I am so grateful for this wonderful food.
My body loves the way I choose the
perfect foods for every meal.
All of my meals are harmonious.
I love taking time to eat mindfully and fully enjoy my meals.
I am well nourished in preparation for the day ahead of me.
My body heals and strengthens with every bite I take.
Mealtimes are happy times.
My family gathers together with great joy and love.
I bless this food and my body with love.
I listen for when I am satisfied and full.
I listen to my body as I eat.
I pay attention to all of my senses when I eat.
This food is healing me.
My taste buds are changing every day—I no
longer crave foods that don't nourish me.
I listen to my appetite and it guides
me with loving, nourishing choices.
I am willing to slow down and
take this time to nourish myself.

FREEDOM IS MY DIVINE RIGHT

We are put on this planet with total freedom of choice. And we make these choices in our minds. No person, place, or thing can think for us if we do not allow it. We are the only person who thinks in our mind. In our minds we have total freedom. What we choose to think and believe can change our current circumstances beyond recognition.

I am free to think wonderful thoughts. I move beyond past limitations into freedom. I am now becoming all that I am created to be.

I Am Open and Receptive to All the Good and Abundance in the Universe

I sit at least once a day with my arms stretched out to the side and say, "I am open and receptive to all the good and abundance in the Universe." It gives me a feeling of expansion.

The Universe can only distribute to me what I have in my consciousness, and I can *always* create more in my consciousness. It is like a cosmic bank. I make mental deposits by increasing my awareness of my own abilities to create. Meditation, treatments, and affirmations are mental deposits. Let's make a habit of making daily deposits.

I Am Safe in the Universe, and All Life Loves and Supports Me

The stars, the moon, and the sun are all operating in perfect Divine right order. There is an order, a rhythm, and a purpose to their pathways. I am part of the Universe; therefore, I know that there is an order, a rhythm, and a purpose to my life. Sometimes my life may seem to be in chaos, and yet in back of the chaos I know there is a Divine order. As I put my mind in order and learn my lessons, the chaos disappears, and then order comes back. I trust that my life is really in perfect Divine right order. All is well in my world.

I LIVE AND DWELL IN THE TOTALITY OF POSSIBILITIES

Repeat with me: "I live and dwell in the totality of possibilities. Where I am there is all good." Think about these words for a minute. *All good*. Not some, not a little bit, but *all good*. When you believe that anything is possible, you open yourself up to answers in every area of your life.

Where we are is the totality of possibilities. It is always up to us individually and collectively. We either have walls around us or take them down and feel safe enough to be totally open to allow all good to come into our lives. Begin to observe yourself objectively. Notice what is going on inside you—how you feel, how you react, what you believe—and allow yourself to observe without comment or judgment. When you can, you will live your life from the totality of possibilities.

I Am Grateful for Life
Now and Forevermore

Deep at the center of my being there is an infinite well of gratitude. I now allow this gratitude to fill my heart, my body, my mind, my consciousness, my very being. This gratitude radiates out from me in all directions, touching everything in my world, and returns to me as more to be grateful for. The more gratitude I feel, the more I am aware that the supply is endless. The use of gratitude makes me feel good; it is an expression of my inner joy. It is a warm fuzzy in my life.

I am grateful for myself and for my body. I am grateful for my ability to see and hear, feel and taste and touch. I am grateful for my home, and I take loving care of it. I am grateful for my family and friends, and I rejoice in their company. I am grateful for my work, and I give it my best at all times. I am grateful for my talents and abilities, and I continually express them in ways that are fulfilling. I am grateful for my income, and I know that I prosper wherever I turn. I am grateful for all my past experiences, for I know that they were part of my soul's growth. I am grateful for all of nature, and I am respectful of every living thing. I am grateful for today, and I am grateful for the tomorrows to come.

I am grateful for Life now and forevermore.

I Give and Receive Gifts Graciously

Appreciation and acceptance act like powerful magnets for miracles every moment of the day. Compliments are gifts of prosperity. I have learned to accept them graciously. If somebody compliments me, I smile and say, "Thank you."

Today is a sacred gift from Life. I open my arms wide to receive the full measure of prosperity that the Universe offers. Any time of the day or night, I can let it in.

The Universe supports me in every way possible. I live in a loving, abundant, harmonious Universe, and I am grateful. There are times in life, however, when the Universe gives to me but I am not in a position to do anything about giving back. I can think of many people who helped me enormously at times when there was no way I could ever repay them. Later, however, I was able to help others, and that's the way life goes. I relax and rejoice in the abundance and gratitude that are here now.

My Later Years Are
My Treasure Years

We want to create a conscious ideal of our later years as the most rewarding phase of our lives. We need to know that our future is always bright no matter what our age. We can do this if we just change our thoughts. It's time to dispel the fearful images of old age. It's time to take a quantum leap in our thinking. We need to take the word *old* out of our vocabulary and become a planet where the long-lived are still young—and where life expectancy isn't given a finite number. We want to see our later years become our treasure years.

We Have a Healing World to Live In

There is so much good I can do for the planet on an individual level. At times I may work for causes, putting my physical energy or finances into them. And at other times I may use the power of my thoughts to help heal the planet. If I hear news of a world disaster or acts of senseless violence, I use my mind in a positive way. I know that if I send angry thoughts toward those responsible, then I am not helping to heal. So I immediately surround the whole situation with love and affirm that out of this experience only good will come. I send positive energy and do visualizations, seeing the incident working out as quickly as possible with a solution that is for the best for everyone. I bless the perpetrators with love and affirm that the part of them where love and compassion dwells comes to the surface and that they too are healed. It is only when we are all healed and whole that we will have a healing world to live in.

My Healing Journey Begins with Kind and Loving Thoughts

Affirmations for Overcoming Dis-ease

I love my body.
My body loves to be healthy.
I appreciate my glorious body.
I listen to my body's messages.
Every cell in my body is loved.
I know how to take care of myself.
I am healthier than I have ever been.
I am in harmony with every part of life.
I lovingly create perfect health for myself.
I give my body what it needs on every level
to bring it to optimal health.

MY GOOD COMES FROM EVERYWHERE AND EVERYONE

In the infinity of life where I am,
all is perfect, whole, and complete.
I am one with the Power that created me.
I am totally open and receptive to the
abundant flow of prosperity that the Universe offers.
All my needs and desires are met before I even ask.
I am Divinely guided and protected,
and I make choices that are beneficial for me.
I rejoice in others' successes,
knowing there is plenty for us all.
I am constantly increasing my conscious
awareness of abundance, and this reflects
in a constantly increasing income.
My good comes from everywhere and everyone.
All is well in my world.

Lifetimes Come and Go, but I Am Always Eternal

I release the past with ease, and I trust the process of life. I close the door on old hurts, and I forgive everyone, myself included. I visualize a stream in front of me. I take all those old experiences, the old hurts and pains, and I put them all into the stream and watch them begin to dissolve and drift downstream until they totally dissipate and disappear. I am free and everyone in my past is free. I am ready to move forward into the new adventures that await me. Lifetimes come and go, but I am always eternal. I am alive and vital, no matter which plane of action I am on. Love surrounds me, now and forevermore. And so it is!

I Draw Love and Romance into My Life, and I Accept It Now

I am one with Life, and all of Life loves and supports me. Therefore, I claim love and intimacy in my world. I am worthy of love. I am not my parents, nor their own relationship patterns. I am my own unique self, and I choose to create and keep a long-lasting, loving relationship—one that nurtures and supports us both in every way. We have great compatibility and similar rhythms, and we bring out the best in each other. We're romantic, and we're the best of friends. I rejoice in this long-term relationship. This is the truth of my being, and I accept it as so. All is well in my loving world.

I AM ALREADY A BEAUTIFUL, SUCCESSFUL PERSON

I have within me all the ingredients for success, just like the acorn has the complete oak tree curled within its tiny form. I set standards that are achievable for where I am right now. I encourage and praise my improvements. It's okay for me to learn from every experience, and it's okay for me to make mistakes while I'm learning. This is the way I move from success to success, and every day it gets a little easier to see things in this light. When failure appears before me, I no longer run away from it; rather, I acknowledge it as a lesson. I give failure no power. There is only One Power in this entire Universe, and this Power is 100 percent successful in everything it does. It created me; therefore, I am already a beautiful, successful person.

Harmony Surrounds Me

We are each a Divine idea expressing through the One Mind in harmonious ways. We have come together because there is something we need to learn from each other. We have a purpose in being together. There is no need to fight this purpose or to blame one another for what is happening. It is safe for us to work on loving ourselves so that we may benefit and grow from this experience. We choose to work together to bring harmony into the business at hand and into every area of our own lives. Everything we do is based on the one truth—the truth of our beings and the truth of Life.

Divine right action is guiding us every moment of the day. We say the right word at the right time and follow the right course of action at all times. Each person is part of the harmonious whole. There is a Divine blending of energies as people work joyfully together, supporting and encouraging each other in ways that are fulfilling and productive. We are successful in every area of our work and our lives. We are healthy, happy, loving, joyful, respectful, supportive, and at peace with ourselves and with each other. So be it, and so it is.

I Move from Poverty Thinking to Prosperity Thinking

Many people worry about the economy and believe they will either earn or lose money due to the economic situation at present. However, the economy is always moving up and down. So, it doesn't matter what is happening out there, or what others do to change the economy. We are not stuck because of the economy. No matter what is happening "out there" in the world, it only matters what you believe about yourself.

If you have a fear about becoming homeless, ask yourself, "Where am I not at home within myself? Where do I feel abandoned? What do I need to do to experience inner peace?" All outer experiences reflect inner beliefs.

I have always used the affirmation *My income is constantly increasing.* Another affirmation I like is *I go beyond my parents' income level.* You have a right to earn more than your parents did. It's almost a necessity since things cost more now. Women, especially, experience a lot of conflict with this one. Often they find it difficult to earn more than their fathers are earning. They need to go beyond their feelings of not deserving and accept the abundance of financial wealth that is their Divine right.

Everything I Touch Is a Success

Many people have negative beliefs about prosperity and money. These are beliefs they learned as children but now that they're adults, they can change these beliefs to better their lives. Let's affirm together: *I now forgive all those in my childhood who, in their ignorance, taught me negative and incorrect things about myself. I love my parents, and I now move beyond their old, limiting thoughts. I now declare that these affirmations are my new and true beliefs about myself and about life. I accept them as truth and know I deserve all good in this world.*

Here are more affirmations for you. It would help to write them on a piece of paper and keep them in areas where you will see them often.

*Today I am wealthy. It is all right if my family
and childhood friends continue to believe in
limiting thoughts. They do not have to grow
in the same way I am growing.*

*There is more money in this world
than there are grains of sand.*

*God loves those who use their talents
and abilities to become rich in loving ways.*

*I do matter—to myself and to Life. I am
deeply loved and cherished by the Universe.*

*As part of my prosperity growth, I am free to move
from one social level to another without guilt or fear.*

THE FIRST WORDS I SAY TO MYSELF EACH DAY ARE *I LOVE YOU*

First thing in the morning and last thing in the evening, I want you to look into your eyes and say: "I love you, I really love you. And I accept you exactly as you are." It can be tough at first, but if you stick with it, in a short time this affirmation will be true for you. Won't that be fun!

You'll find that as your self-love grows, so will your self-respect, and any changes that you find yourself needing to make will be easier to accomplish when you know that they're the right ones for you. Love is never outside yourself—it's always within you. As you're more loving, you'll be more lovable.

So choose new thoughts to think about yourself, and choose new words to tell yourself how magnificent you are and that you deserve all the good that Life has to offer.

I Choose to Make the Rest of My Life the Best of My Life

I now choose to move away from the limiting beliefs that have been denying me the benefits I so desire. I declare that every negative thought pattern in my consciousness is now being cleared out, erased, and let go. My consciousness is now being filled with cheerful, positive, loving thought patterns that contribute to my health, wealth, and loving relationships. I now release all negative patterns that have contributed to fear of loss, fear of the dark, fear of being harmed, or fear of poverty. I also release those that have brought me pain, loneliness, self-abuse, undeservingness, burdens or losses of any sort, and any other nonsense that may be lingering in some dark corner of my consciousness.

I am now free to allow the good to manifest in my life. I declare for myself the richness and fullness of life in all its profuse abundance: love—lavishly flowing; prosperity—abounding; health—vital and vibrant; creativity—ever new and fresh; and peace—all-surrounding. All this I deserve and am now willing to accept and have on a permanent basis. I am a co-creator with the One Infinite Allness of Life, and the totality of possibilities lies before me.

I Am Open and Receptive to New Avenues of Income

We want to release the "fixed income" mentality. Do not limit the Universe by insisting that you have "only" a certain salary or income. That salary or income is a *channel*; it is not your *source*. Your supply comes from one source, the Universe itself.

There are an infinite number of channels. We must open ourselves to them. We must accept in consciousness that supply can come from anywhere and everywhere. Then when we walk down the street and find a penny or a dime, we say "Thank you!" to the source. It may be small, but new channels are beginning to open.

I am open and receptive to new avenues of income.

*I now receive my good from
expected and unexpected sources.*

*I am an unlimited being accepting from
an unlimited source in an unlimited way.*

I LOVE MY MIND AND MY MIND LOVES ME

Stop for a moment and catch your thought. What are you thinking right now? If thoughts shape your life and experiences, would you want this thought to become true for you? If it's a thought of worry, anger, hurt, or revenge, how do you think that this thought will come back for you? If we want a joyous life, we must think joyous thoughts. Whatever we send out mentally or verbally will come back to us in like form.

Take a little time to listen to the words you say. If you hear yourself saying something three times, write it down. It has become a pattern for you. At the end of a week, look at the list you've made and you'll see how your words fit your experiences. Be willing to change your words and thoughts, and watch your life change. The way to control your life is to control your choice of words and thoughts. No one thinks in your mind but you.

I DESERVE TO FEEL GOOD

Life is very simple. We create our experiences by our patterns of thought and feeling. What we believe about ourselves and about life becomes true for us. Thoughts are only words strung together. They have no meaning whatsoever. It is we who give meaning to them. We give meaning to them by focusing on the negative messages over and over in our minds.

What we do with our feelings is very important. Are we going to act them out? Will we punish others? Sadness, loneliness, guilt, anger, and fear are all normal emotions. But when these feelings take over and become predominant, life can be an emotional battlefield.

Through mirror work, self-love, and positive affirmations, you can nourish yourself and relieve any of the anxiety you may be feeling at the moment. Do you believe you deserve peace and serenity in your emotional life?

Let's affirm: *I release the pattern in my consciousness that is creating resistance to my good. I deserve to feel good.*

I RISE ABOVE ALL LIMITATIONS

I envelop my entire family in a circle of love—those who are living and those who are dead. I affirm wonderful, harmonious experiences that are meaningful for all of us. I feel so blessed to be part of the timeless web of unconditional love that brings us all together. Ancestors who lived before me did the best they could with the knowledge and understanding they had, and children not yet born will face new challenges and will do the best they can with the knowledge and understanding they will have. Each day I see my task more clearly, which is simply to let go of old family limitations and awaken to Divine harmony.

I Am Grown Up Now, and I Take Loving Care of My Inner Child

Affirmations for Nurturing the Inner Child

I love myself totally in the now.
I embrace my inner child with love.
I am willing to go beyond my own limitations.
I take responsibility for my own life. I am free.
I am grown up now, and I take
loving care of my inner child.
I now go beyond my old fears and limitations.
I am at peace with myself and my life.
I am safe to express my feelings.
I love and approve of myself.
I create my future now.

Only Good Lies Before Me

When you spend time with Louise Hay, you get to see that she doesn't just think about affirmations; she lives her affirmations. She doesn't just do 10 minutes of affirmations in the morning and then get on with her day. She takes her affirmations with her all through the day. To help, she has affirmations discreetly placed around her home. Affirmations like *Life loves me* on her bathroom mirror; *All is well* by a light switch in the hall; and *Only good lies before me* on her kitchen wall. One in her car reads, *I bless and prosper everyone in my life, and everyone in my life blesses and prospers me.*

I Relax, Knowing That Life Supports Me at All Times

I am neither lonely nor abandoned in the Universe. All of Life supports me every moment of the day and night. Everything I need for a fulfilling life is already provided for me. There is enough breath to last me for as long as I shall live. The earth is supplied with an abundance of food. There are millions of people to interact with. I am supported in every possible way.

Every thought I think is mirrored for me in my experiences. Life always says yes to me. All I need do is accept this abundance and support with joy and pleasure and gratitude. I now release from within my consciousness any and all patterns or beliefs that would deny me my good. I am loved and supported by Life itself.

WE ARE HERE TO BLESS AND PROSPER EACH OTHER

One of the ways to attract money into your life is to tithe, or donate. Tithing 10 percent of your income has long been an established principle. I like to think of it as giving back to Life. When we do that, we seem to prosper more.

Who or what has nourished you on your quest for improving the quality of your life? That could be the perfect place for you to tithe. If tithing to a church or a person doesn't appeal to you, there are many wonderful nonprofit organizations that could benefit others by your contributions. Investigate and find the one that is right for you. People often say, "I will tithe when I have more money." Of course then they never do. If you are going to tithe, start now and watch the blessings flow. However, if you only tithe to get more, then you have missed the point. It must be freely given or it won't work. I feel that life has been good to me and I gladly give to life in various ways.

I Live in a *Yes* Universe

I've learned that there are really just two mental patterns that contribute to dis-ease: fear and anger. Anger can show up as impatience, irritation, frustration, criticism, resentment, jealousy, or bitterness. These are all thoughts that poison the body. When we release this burden, all the organs in our body begin to function properly. Fear could be tension, anxiety, nervousness, worry, doubt, insecurity, feeling not good enough, or unworthiness. Do you relate to any of this stuff? We must learn to substitute faith for fear if we are to heal.

Faith in what? Faith in life. I believe that we live in a *yes* Universe. No matter what we choose to believe or think, the Universe always says *yes* to us. If we think poverty, the Universe says *yes* to that. If we think prosperity, the Universe says *yes* to that. So we want to think and believe that we have the right to be healthy, that health is natural to us. The Universe will support and say *yes* to this belief. Be a *yes* person, and know that you live in a *yes* world, being responded to by a *yes* Universe.

I LOVE THE PLANET

Envision the world as a great place to live in. See disease become a thing of the past, and all the hospitals now apartment buildings. See prison inmates being taught how to love themselves and being released as responsible citizens. See churches remove sin and guilt from their teachings. See governments really taking care of people.

Go outside and feel the clean rain falling. As the rain stops, see a beautiful rainbow appear. Notice the sun shining. Smell the fresh clean air. See the water glisten and sparkle in our rivers, streams, and lakes. And notice the lush vegetation. Forests filled with trees. Flowers, fruits, and vegetables abundant and available everywhere.

Go to other countries and see peace and plenty for all. See harmony between all people as we lay down our guns. Judgment, criticism, and prejudice become archaic and fade away. See borders crumbling and separateness disappearing. See all of us becoming one. See our Mother Earth, the planet, healed and whole.

You are creating this new world now, just by using your mind to envision a new world. You are powerful. You are important, and you do count. Live your vision. Go out and do what you can to make this vision come true. God bless us all. And so it is.

I Love Myself and Others and Allow Others to Love Me

Let's open our hearts so that we can take in everyone with love, support, and caring. Let's move that love to people in the street who have no homes and no place to go. Let's share our love with those who are angry, frightened, or in pain. Let's send love to the people who are in the process of leaving the planet and those who have already left.

Let's share our love with everybody, whether they accept it or not. Let's hold the entire planet in our hearts: the animals, the vegetation, and all the people. The people we are angry at or frustrated with. Those who are not doing things our way. And those who are expressing so-called evil—let's take them into our hearts, too, so that from a feeling of safety they can begin to recognize who they really are.

See peace breaking out all over the planet. Know that you are contributing to that peace right now. Rejoice that you have the ability to do something positive to help. Acknowledge how wonderful you are. Know that it is the truth for you. And so it is.

THIS WORLD IS OUR HEAVEN ON EARTH

We are a community of spiritually minded souls who come together to share, grow, and radiate our energies into the world—each one free to pursue his or her activity and drawn together to better fulfill each individual's purpose. We are guided to form the new Heaven on Earth with others who have the same desire to prove to themselves and others that it can be now.

We live together harmoniously, lovingly, and peacefully—expressing God in our lives and in our living. We establish a world where the nurturing of soul growth is the most important activity, and where this is the work of the individual. There is ample time and opportunity for creative expression in whatever area we choose. All that we need we will be able to express through the powers within. There is no dis-ease, no poverty, no crime, and no deceit. The world of the future begins now, right here, with all of us. And so it is.

All Is Well in My World

In the infinity of life where I am,
all is perfect, whole, and complete.
Each one of us, myself included,
experiences the richness and fullness
of life in ways that are meaningful to us.
I now look at the past with love and choose
to learn from my old experiences.
There is no right or wrong, nor good or bad.
The past is over and done.
There is only the experience of the moment.
I love myself for bringing myself
through this past into this present moment.
I share what and who I am,
for I know we are all one in Spirit.
All is well in my world.

I See the World Becoming an Incredible Circle of Love

Think of today and every day as a time of learning, a new beginning. It is an opportunity to change and grow, to open your consciousness to a new level and consider new ideas and new ways of thinking, to envision the world we dream of living in. Our vision helps to create the world.

I Am a Radiant Being of Love

Deep at the center of my being there is an infinite supply of love. It is inexhaustible. I can never use it all in this lifetime, so I don't have to be sparing with it. I can always be generous with my love. Love is contagious. When I share love, it comes back to me multiplied. The more love I give, the more love I have. I have come to this world to be a love giver. I came in full of love. And even though I will share my love all my life, when I leave this earth I will still have a full and happy heart. If I want more love, then I have only to give love. Love is, and I am.

I Let the Spirit of Love Flow through Me Today

Go back in time and remember the very best Christmas you ever had as a child. Bring the memory up in your mind and see it very clearly. Remember the sights, the smells, the tastes and touches, and the people who were there. What were some of the things that you did? If perchance you never had a wonderful Christmas as a child, make one up. Make it exactly as you would like it to be.

As you think of this special Christmas, notice that your heart is opening. Perhaps one of the most wonderful things about that particular Christmas was the love that was present. Let the spirit of love flow through you now. Bring into your heart all the people you know and care about. Surround them with this love.

Know that you can carry this special feeling of Christmas love and spirit with you everywhere and have it all the time, not only at Christmas. You are love. You are Spirit. You are light. You are energy. And so it is.

I HAVE ENOUGH LOVE IN MY HEART TO HEAL THE WHOLE PLANET

There is enough love in you to love the whole planet, and it starts with you. Begin by affirming *Life loves me, and I love life*. Say it out loud. Say it a few times. Complete the sentence *One way life is loving me right now is . . .* Count your blessings. If you find this difficult, affirm that you are willing to receive and that you are open to all offers of help. Affirm: *Today I move into my greater good. My good is everywhere, and I am safe and secure.*

Wish everyone you love a beautiful day today. Affirm for them: *Life loves you.* Pray that they may know how blessed they are and that they recognize the basic truth about themselves, which is *I am lovable.* Be happy for their success, their abundance, their good health, and their good fortune. Remember, if you want love and acceptance from your family, then you must have love and acceptance for them. Affirm: *I rejoice in everyone's happiness, knowing that there is plenty for us all.*

LIFE LOVES US, AND I WISH EVERYONE INFINITE BLESSINGS TODAY

Set up in your mind that you will bless everyone you meet today. Send a blessing to all your neighbors on both sides of the street. Send a blessing to all the parents you normally see at the school gate. Send a blessing to the local shopkeeper, to the mailman, to the bus driver, and to every other familiar face in your community. Send a blessing to the trees on your street. Send a blessing to your entire neighborhood. Affirm: *Life loves you and I wish you infinite blessings today.*

Send a blessing to the people you're tempted to withhold love from. Bless the person you judge the most and affirm: *Life loves us all.* Bless the person you fight with the most and affirm: *Life loves us all.* Bless the person you complain about the most and affirm: *Life loves us all.* Bless the person you envy the most and affirm: *Life loves us all.* Bless the person you compete with the most and affirm: *Life loves us all.* Bless your enemies, so that you have no enemies. Affirm: *We are all lovable. Life loves us all. In love, everyone wins.*

I See the World through Eyes of Love and Acceptance

You are important, and what you do with your mind makes a difference. Send out a blessing to the whole world every day. When you affirm *Life loves me, and I love life*, you paint in your consciousness an unbroken circle of receiving and giving. *Life loves me* represents the receiving principle, and *I love life* represents the giving principle. The full affirmation supports you in receiving and giving love in equal measure. In truth, giving *is* receiving. The giver and the receiver are the same person. What you give, you receive. And what you receive, you can give. This awareness is what helps you to be a truly loving presence in the world.

Affirm: *Life loves me, and I love life.* Imagine that you hold the whole planet in your heart. Love the animals. Love the plants. Love the oceans. Love the stars. Visualize newspaper headlines like "An End to Poverty" or "Peace on Earth." Each time you bless the world with your love, you connect with millions of people doing the same thing. See the world evolving in the direction of love today. Affirm: *Together we are creating a world in which it is safe to love one another.*

I AM SAFE AND SECURE AS I MOVE FORWARD TO MY HIGHEST GOOD

The past is over and done. It has gone back to the nothingness from whence it came. I am free. I have a new sense of pride and self-worth. I am confident in my abilities to love and support myself. I have learned that I am capable of positive growth and change. I am strong. I am united with all of Life. I am one with the Universal Power and Intelligence. Divine Wisdom leads me and guides me every step of the way. I am safe and secure as I move forward to my highest good. I do this with ease and with joy. I am a new person, living in a world of my choosing. I am deeply grateful for all that I have and for all that I am. I am blessed and prosperous in every way. All is well in my world.

I Am Open and Receptive to My Next Step in Life

It doesn't matter how long we've had negative patterns, an illness, a rotten relationship, lack of finances, or self-hatred. Right here and right now in our minds, we can begin to make a change today. The thoughts we've held and the words we've repeatedly used have created our life and experiences up to this point. Yet that is past thinking; we've already done that. What we're choosing to think and say, today, at this moment, will create tomorrow and the next day and the next week and the next month and the next year, and so on. The point of power is always in the present moment. This is where we begin to make changes. What a liberating idea. We can begin to let the old nonsense go. Right now. The smallest beginning will make a difference.

I LOVE LIFE, AND LIFE LOVES ME

This is my love story. I only choose thoughts that create a wonderful future, and I move into it now. My heart is opening wider and wider. Love flows from and to me in ever-increasing amounts. Unconditional love and acceptance are the greatest gifts I can give and receive—and I give them to myself now. I am learning the secrets of Life. It is actually all very simple: The more I love myself, the more I feel Life loving me. The more I love myself, the healthier I am. The more I love myself, the more enjoyable my life gets.

I give myself the green light to go ahead, and I joyously embrace my new, loving habits of food and thoughts. The more I nourish myself, the more I am grateful to be alive. It is my joy and pleasure to live another wonderful day. Every person on this planet is interconnected with love, and it starts with me loving myself. I send loving thoughts to all. Love and forgiveness heals me and it heals us all. My life is balanced, and my immunity is strong. I am healthy, whole, and healed. I love Life, and Life loves me.

ABOUT THE AUTHOR

Louise Hay was an inspirational teacher who educated millions since the 1984 publication of her bestseller *You Can Heal Your Life*, which has more than 50 million copies in print worldwide. Renowned for demonstrating the power of affirmations to bring about positive change, Louise was the author of more than 30 books for adults and children, including the bestsellers *The Power Is Within You* and *Heal Your Body*. In addition to her books, Louise produced numerous audio and video programs, card decks, online courses, and other resources for leading a healthy, joyous, and fulfilling life.

Websites: www.louisehay.com,
www.healyourlife.com, and
www.facebook.com/louiselhay

Hay House Titles of Related Interest

We hope you enjoyed this Hay House book. If you'd like to receive our online catalog featuring additional information on Hay House books and products, or if you'd like to find out more about the Hay Foundation, please contact:

Hay House, Inc., P.O. Box 5100, Carlsbad, CA 92018-5100
(760) 431-7695 or (800) 654-5126
(760) 431-6948 (fax) or (800) 650-5115 (fax)
www.hayhouse.com® • www.hayfoundation.org

———

Published in Australia by:
Hay House Australia Pty. Ltd., 18/36 Ralph St., Alexandria NSW 2015
Phone: 612-9669-4299 • *Fax:* 612-9669-4144 • www.hayhouse.com.au

Published in the United Kingdom by:
Hay House UK, Ltd., Astley House, 33 Notting Hill Gate, London W11 3JQ
Phone: 44-20-3675-2450 • *Fax:* 44-20-3675-2451 • www.hayhouse.co.uk

Published in India by: Hay House Publishers India,
Muskaan Complex, Plot No. 3, B-2, Vasant Kunj, New Delhi 110 070
Phone: 91-11-4176-1620 • *Fax:* 91-11-4176-1630 • www.hayhouse.co.in

———

Access New Knowledge.
Anytime. Anywhere.

Learn and evolve at your own pace
with the world's leading experts.

www.hayhouseU.com